Reflections On Conducting
Hilary Davan Wetton

First published in 2021 by Queen's Temple Publications
Printed and bound by Caligraving Ltd
Cover photograph by Karen Parker
Design by Helen Tabor
Copyright © 2021 by Queen's Temple Publications
All rights reserved

ISBN 978-1-3999-1067-5

QT205

No part of this book may be reproduced by any mechanical, photographic, or electronic process, or in the form of a phonographic recording, nor may it be stored in a retrieval system, transmitted, or otherwise copied for public or private use without the written permission of the publisher.

Queen's Temple Publications

Contents

4	Biography
5	Preface by Alan Rusbridger
7	Foreword
8	Starting Out
11	Technique
16	Preparation
21	Programme Planning
26	Performance and Presentation
30	Rehearsals
39	Choral Conducting
46	Orchestral Accompaniment
52	Touring
57	Youth Orchestras
63	Guest Conducting
68	Opera and Ballet
72	Recording
75	Contemporary Composers
80	The Conductor and the Audience
85	Odds and Ends
90	Coda
92	Acknowledgements
93	Discography

HILARY DAVAN WETTON has enjoyed a wide-ranging career as a conductor both of choirs and orchestras. Musical Director of the City of London Choir (CLC) since 1989, he was conductor of the Guildford Choral Society (GCS) from 1968-2008, Artistic Director of the Leicester Philharmonic Choir from 2009-2018 and Founder Conductor of the Holst Singers from 1979-1993. He has worked with many British orchestras as well as orchestras in Europe, Australia and the US. Artistic Director of the Milton Keynes City Orchestra (MKCO) from 1975-2008, he was also Conductor of the Wren Orchestra of London for ten years. He is currently Associate Conductor of the London Mozart Players and Artistic Director of the Military Wives Choirs.

A lifelong commitment to youth music has included posts as conductor of the Birmingham Schools' Symphony Orchestra, Edinburgh Youth Orchestra and the Orchestra of the Royal Birmingham Conservatoire. He has also been Professor of Conducting at the Guildhall School of Music and Drama and Senior Music Associate at Somerville College, Oxford.

Hilary's extensive discography includes award-winning recordings of Holst's *The Planets* with the London Philharmonic Orchestra, Beethoven's *Der Glorreiche Augenblick* with the CLC and the Royal Philharmonic Orchestra (RPO) and Holst's *The Evening Watch* with the Holst Singers. His 1993 recording of Holst's *Choral Symphony* with the GCS and the RPO was awarded the Diapason d'Or. With the MKCO, he made first recordings of neglected English symphonies by Samuel Wesley, William Crotch, Sterndale Bennett and Cipriani Potter which are widely admired. *Flowers of the Field* (Naxos) was released on Remembrance Day 2014 and went straight to the top of the specialist classical charts. Hilary's recording with the Military Wives Choirs, *Remember*, released on Remembrance Day 2018, was also listed in the classical charts for several weeks.

Hilary came to wide public notice through his Classic FM programme *Masterclass*, where he introduced major orchestral works with a live orchestra. He was also Jo Brand's organ tutor for the BBC1 series *Play it Again*. An honorary fellow of the Royal Birmingham Conservatoire, he has been awarded honorary degrees by the Open University and De Montfort University.

Preface by Alan Rusbridger

Our lives are often shaped by chance. It was my good fortune, as a keenly musical thirteen-year-old, to arrive at my secondary school at the same time as Hilary Davan Wetton was appointed to run the music department. It was, I now see, a daring appointment. Tall, wiry and with a boyish mop of hair, Hilary could have passed as a sixth-former: he was still only twenty-three. He also had a youthful enthusiasm and energy – along with a capability for retrieving last-minute order out of apparent chaos.

His ambition was boundless. At other schools they might perform a handful of choruses from Handel's *Messiah*. Hilary mounted a production of Mussorgsky's sprawling opera, *Boris Godunov*. Amateur orchestras conventionally survived on a diet of Haydn and early Beethoven; Hilary staged Verdi's Requiem. As a fourteen-year-old clarinettist I found myself playing Tchaikovsky symphonies alongside professionals down for the day from London.

Looking back across half a century or more, I'm not entirely sure how it all happened. Hilary's office looked as though a tornado had recently blasted through it. In addition to training voices and instruments he seemed to single-handedly book halls, soloists and entire orchestras. Yet, on the day, everything magically fell into place.

Even today I can remember the thrill of playing the bass drum in Verdi's Requiem and the cymbals in Vaughan Williams's heaving *A Sea Symphony*. I played percussion in Orff's *Carmina Burana*; sang in oratorios; performed Mozart's clarinet concerto; and – much later – sang in the Royal Albert Hall in a birthday performance of Elgar's *The Dream of Gerontius*.

By then I was editor of *The Guardian* newspaper and Hilary was marking his seventieth birthday – and fifty years or more of conducting orchestras and choirs around the country and abroad. He had become known for championing English music – I first performed Vaughan Williams, Delius, Holst and Butterworth under his baton – and he had built up a considerable reputation for inspiring amateur forces.

Of course, Hilary had also worked with many professional orchestras and choirs. But he had a special skill for inspiring amateurs to perform works they might have considered impossible. He coached, coaxed, cajoled and energised amateur forces into performing out of their skins. He gave them experiences they would never forget.

At the grand age of seventy-seven – but still looking improbably boyish – Hilary has put his enforced pandemic sabbatical to good use by writing about his particular talent at the podium. When I first met him he was still digesting the experience of studying with Sir Adrian Boult: a restrained, Edwardian school of conducting (Boult had given his first classes in 1919). By the time Hilary recently came to work with the choir of Lady Margaret Hall, Oxford, where I was by then Principal, his style had changed greatly from those early days of using an improbably long Boultian baton, with rubber bands around the grip, the better to control the understated rotation of the fingers. But he was still the same old Hilary – knowing exactly what had to be done in never-enough time to produce a memorable performance of Duruflé's Requiem.

Great conductors famously have age-defying properties, and it is to be hoped that Hilary will continue to enthuse choirs and orchestras for many years to come. Meanwhile, this volume should help inspire future generations of conductors to emulate a musical life well spent.

Foreword

There are already a large number of books about conducting, full of wisdom and advice for young conductors. It might well be asked, 'what need there is for another such book?' My excuse is two-fold: having conducted my first concert sixty years ago provides some perspective on the nature of the role over the last two generations and the particular mix of professional, amateur and student groups with which I have worked has helped me to understand both the differences and the many similarities between the three.

This book is an attempt to define some of the necessary ingredients in developing a conducting career and an account of the methods of various conductors I have known and observed in action. By far the greatest influence on my conducting has been Sir Adrian Boult, perhaps the greatest British conductor of the twentieth century, whose combination of musical and technical skill gave him an extraordinary authority on the podium. He was also a man of great kindness and generosity, despite having an uncontrollable temper that could occasionally explode all over an orchestra, a choir or a student (I speak from experience).

To be a successful conductor requires a range of abilities and capabilities. Musical skills, organisational skills and management skills need to be combined with a passion for the music you seek to communicate and a deep respect for the musicians with whom you collaborate. Luck too, is an essential requirement; I know several fine conductors whose careers have failed simply because they were never in the right place at the right time.

I hope that this book, intended though it is for the general reader, may also be helpful to the student conductor. There are those who believe that you cannot teach conducting; I do not share that view. No teacher can create a conductor, but there are obvious pitfalls – technical, musical and personal – that a student can avoid if happy to learn from more than experience alone.

Both Boult and Sir Henry Wood, the founder of the BBC Proms, produced daunting lists of the qualifications they believed were required to become a conductor. They implied that you need to be a cross between Mozart and the Angel Gabriel to have any chance of having a successful career in the profession. Thankfully, that has not been my experience. I have had failures and successes, steered down a number of cul-de-sacs and had the occasional stroke of good fortune, which enables me to say in all honesty that if I were to see my career publicly advertised, I would probably apply for it. To have been paid to do what you enjoy at least ninety per cent of the time is a massive privilege and I am hugely grateful to all my colleagues, both amateur and professional, who have sustained that percentage for so long at so high a level.

Starting Out

There is no set template for preparing to be a conductor. Sir Simon Rattle came to conducting via the percussion section of the Merseyside Youth Orchestra; Lorin Maazel was a child violin prodigy. Some conductors, Sir John Barbirolli and Bernard Haitink, for example, graduated from an orchestral background; others, like Sir Andrew Davis, did so from the organ loft.

Most of us, however, become conductors as much by chance as by design. I became obsessed with the organ while at Westminster School, where our daily service in Westminster Abbey made a profound impression. The school was not particularly musical, although its then Director of Music, Arnold Foster, was a friend of Vaughan Williams and also introduced me to Orff's *Carmina Burana* long before it became fashionable. I left school at sixteen, rather to my father's alarm, to study the organ at the Royal College of Music (RCM). I was allocated the great Sir George Thalben-Ball as my teacher; the piano was my second study.

At the end of my first term I had found the piano so boring that I went to talk to the registrar about what I might study in its place. He told me that the RCM was about to reintroduce a conducting class after a gap of some years. 'You might find it useful to learn basic conducting if you want to be an organist,' he said. By this stage I had already acquired my first musical position – as organist at Her Majesty's Prison, Brixton. I was not invited to conduct the prisoners and the novelty of bicycling two round trips of twelve miles each Sunday to play four services for half a guinea a time was wearing off. Soon afterwards, however, I acquired a more congenial post at St Mary's Church in West Kensington so that my first choir practices happily coincided with my first lessons in conducting.

There were six of us in the RCM conducting class. We were allocated twenty minutes every other week with the second orchestra – a luxury by modern standards. Our tutor, Harvey Phillips, best known as a 'cellist, was in charge of that orchestra. He was a kindly and thoughtful man who chain-smoked throughout our classes but was otherwise delightful. At our first rehearsal he called for volunteers to conduct Franck's Symphony in D minor, of which we had acquired scores only a day or two before. With astonishing rashness – and absolutely no idea of what was involved – I put myself forward. Luckily, the orchestra was tolerant and enabled me to delude myself that I was in charge. The first flute was a friend; she said afterwards that she could at least see my stick (one colleague had beaten consistently below the level of the music stand), but that it was a shame she had not once seen my eyes!

I conducted my first public concert at Easter 1961, a performance of Handel's *Messiah* in St Mary's Church. I am relieved that there is no recording of this event, but it was hugely exciting for me, of course. The orchestra was led by Diana Cummings (then leader of the orchestra of the Royal Academy of Music). So began a happy collaboration that lasted over fifty years. All conductors, unless they are themselves skilled violinists, need ruthlessly to steal ideas from their leaders. Most leaders are happy to give advice and to demonstrate alternative possibilities in rehearsal; never underestimate the importance of the leader to a conductor.

Study at Oxford University followed. Here it was possible to conduct five or six concerts a term, providing one was not too self-critical or too devoted to one's academic work. Though standards were variable and rehearsal attendance sketchy, it was a wonderful way to learn repertoire in a protected setting. Though I found the academic music course unrewarding most of the time (there were no performance options), I learned a great deal about rehearsing, programme planning and recruiting an audience through 'experience-based learning'! These experiences have proved invaluable since; it is good to be exposed to the practical aspects of promoting concerts as part of one's apprenticeship as a conductor.

There was no formal conducting instruction available in the university but I was sensible enough to go twice to the Canford Summer School where the charismatic George Hurst directed a large and diverse conducting class. He was authoritarian and dogmatic as a teacher but, fundamentally, kind and encouraging. More importantly, he had a clear and flexible technique that you were expected to emulate. He was also inspiring – clearly an important quality in a teacher. Though I only worked with him for two weeks, separated by two years, I learnt more from him than I did from Harvey Phillips in a year. The danger of his method, which was certainly effective, was that it gave his students the impression that conducting was mainly about technique and discussion about musical issues was not encouraged. Nonetheless, he undoubtedly helped me to be a better conductor at the end of my Oxford career and certainly helped me to acquire my first permanent relationship with one of the university orchestras. He also made it possible for me to attend two or three of his rehearsals at the BBC Proms, where his very efficient time-management made a strong impression on me.

In my final year at Oxford the Royal Philharmonic Orchestra (RPO) made a visit to the New Theatre on a Sunday in March. The orchestra was in dire financial straits at the time (a regular condition for most British orchestras throughout my career). Sir Thomas Beecham, its founder, had died four years earlier, leaving no support for the RPO. They were desperately trying to survive by playing anywhere they could – the Odeon Cinema in London's Swiss Cottage and miscellaneous provincial theatres included. Sir Adrian Boult was to conduct Brahms' Symphony No. 4, Op. 98, which I had got to know well the previous year. On a whim, I decided to go. I was treated to a lesson in conducting that was like a Damascene conversion. Boult had studied the Brahms symphonies with Hans Richter, who had performed them in front of the composer; the authority Boult brought to this performance on a wet Sunday afternoon was breath-taking. On the one occasion when his baton lifted over his shoulder, I thought the ceiling would blow off. In a lather of excitement, I wrote a card asking if I might study with him and handed it in at the Randolph Hotel, where he was staying. The porter put it under Boult's door: characteristically he wrote back the very next day, inviting me to join his class at the RCM to which he was returning in the autumn. I was lucky to be able to do exactly that.

Boult was an imposing figure. Tall and upright, he looked – and sounded – a bit like an army colonel. Underneath was a musician of exceptional aural ability and white-hot passion. To watch him conducting, with the controlled stick technique he had developed over decades, gave an impression of an intellectual, detached interpreter. This was wholly false, as those who could see his face, and in particular his eyes, would testify. He caused me to reexamine my own technique almost from scratch; his deputy – Vernon 'Tod' Handley – had refined the Boult technique even further and from him I learned such ideas as a 'double-click' to achieve clean pizzicatos. Tod did not quite have Boult's depth of musical culture, but his technique was extraordinary.

For two years I was back at the RCM, for one day a week. It was now not the second but the third orchestra for the 'Advanced' conducting class, but we still had an opportunity to conduct the orchestra almost every week. No conservatoire in the UK is currently able to offer this level of practical experience. I lived in St Albans, where I was Head of Music at St Albans School, worked in the cathedral with Peter Hurford, and played the organ in two local churches. Peter was immensely kind, inviting me to deputise with his St Albans Bach Choir and play continuo for his performances, including a very early broadcast of Monteverdi's Vespers. But it was a casual visit to a local pub, where I met the retiring conductor of the St Albans Choral Society that led to my first appointment as a permanent conductor. The post was initially unpaid: having a young family, I hesitated for a moment, but then decided it was too good to decline. That was the right decision: in the two years I worked with the choir, I was able to conduct Handel's *Messiah*, Haydn's *Nelson Mass*; Britten's *Saint Nicolas*; and several Bach cantatas, among other repertoire; and to learn a great deal about how to motivate mixed-ability and mixed-aged singers to work hard together.

To conclude, I would like to offer a few guidelines for the aspiring conductor:

1. Immerse yourself in every possible way of making music, as often as possible.

2. Regard every concert or rehearsal you attend as a vital learning experience; go whenever you have the time and can obtain a ticket or pass.

3. Read and prepare scores, even when you have no obvious chance to conduct them. (Tod Handley had a repertoire of several hundred scores before he was offered a professional engagement.)

4. Encourage orchestra and choir members to offer you advice when you work with them.

5. In the early part of your career, accept opportunities to conduct without too much concern for the financial rewards. If you are successful as a conductor, you will be relatively well paid; early opportunities increase the likelihood of that success, so avoid pricing yourself out of an engagement.

Technique

Conducting technique is not a matter upon which there is universal consensus. There are conventions about the patterns with which a conductor indicates the number of beats in a bar and a general agreement that a smaller beat implies a quieter sound than a larger one. Beyond this, there are multiple views about the grip of the stick; the degree of flexibility in the joints of the fingers, the wrist, the elbow and the shoulder; and ultimately, the involvement of the whole body in gesture – or not.

Use of the baton

Sir Adrian Boult was clear that the conductor's baton should be held with the thumb on top and two fingers underneath. It should be driven by the fingers first with a bit of help from the wrist and then the elbow should only be brought into play for the dynamic mezzo forte and above. The shoulder was scarcely used below fortissimo so that the entire range of movement was more controlled than is usual nowadays. That said, he used a very long stick which meant that the movement of the point between beats was quite substantial, despite the limited movement of the arm; 'high gearing' is how he described it and he certainly achieved more subtlety than any of his contemporaries. Of course, he had double-jointed fingers which enabled him to describe a 360-degree circle with the stick without moving his arm; this is a very useful ability, but one that eludes most of us.

I am still convinced that it is right to add each joint of the arm in succession as the dynamic increases. There is something very wearing about a conductor who beats vigorously with the whole arm throughout a passage of mezzo piano or mezzo forte, particularly if the left arm continuously mirrors the right, something that will not assist any choir or orchestra. An even more unhelpful movement is to bend at the knee either at the beginning of each bar or, worse, even more often than that. It may create a great sense of energy for the conductor but it looks unfailingly ridiculous and weakens the transmission of the pulse to the musicians.

There has been a growing tendency for conductors to move around on the rostrum. Some very great conductors – for example, Leonard Bernstein – did this, but however much pleasure it gave the audience to see a 'Lenny Leap', it is very unlikely to have helped the players do their job more successfully. Stillness on the rostrum helps to focus the performers attention on the conductor. If the stick 'clicks' on the pulse on a sight line, drawn more or less from the conductor's sternum to the players, that is likely to be most visible and helpful for those looking for guidance from it. It is also wise to ensure that the stick points directly towards the centre of the orchestra and not at a right angle to it. Some conductors point the stick virtually towards the leader; this is clearly not helpful for the orchestra as a whole.

Of course, it is entirely possible to conduct without a baton. My own experience has been that in a small choral group or an instrumental ensemble fewer than twenty players, the fingers can be more expressive than even a well-controlled stick. As the ensemble gets bigger, visibility becomes a more serious issue. Conducting students are well advised to sit facing the podium in some rehearsals or concerts so they can analyse how much security they can obtain by close attention to the conductor. It is not helpful to judge a conductor from the back – much as the less sophisticated members of the audience may be inclined to do so.

The principle behind the manipulation of the stick is to make it as easy as possible for your collaborators to understand your intentions. There are many studies that show that musicians often find conductors a source of stress. This is exactly the opposite of what should be the case; the conductor should provide unequivocal guidance and a resolute sense of confidence in the success of the performance. The beat needs to be not merely unequivocal but also expressive. Too often, one can observe a laboured, heavy beat failing to extract a beautiful cantabile line from a string section. Good ensembles will compensate for a mismatch between what they see and what they know to be the shape or the dynamic of the phrase, but conductors fail when they pass the responsibility back to the players when it should really be theirs. A number of well-known conductors extract beautiful phrasing without showing it with their sticks, but their rehearsals would clearly be more productive if the beat unequivocally expressed their musical intentions.

It is not easy to describe what makes a stick 'expressive'. A sharp click obviously helps to convey staccato; a legato line is more difficult to do, particularly when an observable pulse on the beat has to be followed by a smooth movement. Boult recommended stroking a table with the stick to cultivate the feel of a click followed by a slide within the beat; acquiring this skill requires considerable practice for most of us. The smaller the beat, the harder it is to produce a legato at a moderate or slow tempo; allowing the beat to move in a more sideways manner can provide useful extra space to keep the stick in motion. The stick does not, of course, move at a constant speed. It has to accelerate towards the pulse so that everybody in the room has a sense of where the beat is arriving. Breathing before the beginning of a new phrase is something many conductors forget to do – it will be helpful both for the ensemble and to help the music retain a singing quality.

The key issue for the conductor is the space *between* the beats, rather than the beats themselves. It is very useful to practise driving the stick from one beat to the other with different speeds of accelerando to the moment of impulse (the quicker the stick movement, the sharper the click will become) and also to practise accelerando and rallentando within two or three beats to ensure that one does not arrive a little too early or late as the pulse changes.

In general terms, the stick should not stop dead except at a fermata. If the music is moving, to arrest the stick will break the line. Of course, it is true that singers and instrumentalists will compensate for counter-productive gestures but they should not have to! Re-starting after a pause can be awkward. The best way to deal with that is to move the stick slowly a little further away from where the next beat will come while holding the pause with the left hand, so that a preparatory movement can indicate clearly where the next pulse is as the music starts again.

Establishing tempo

The preparatory gesture is the key to establishing unequivocally the tempo that is in your head. An 'upbeat' needs to be prepared in the mind, perhaps with a complete internal bar before any movement. Of course, starting in the middle of a bar is marginally more awkward than starting at the beginning of one. To begin in the middle of a beat is a further test of clarity and requires a click that unmistakably indicates the tempo of the anticipatory pulse. Sometimes, one will require two preparatory clicks before a tricky off-beat opening. In that case, the first click needs to have much less impulse than the second. I once observed George Hurst – excellent conductor though he was – start the last movement of Mozart's *Eine Kleine Nachtmusik* in such a way that there was a canon within the first violin section. Clearly, some were expecting two preparatory clicks and others one, and the first click had enough energy to start the more impetuous violinists on their way a beat early! It took about eight bars to get things back onto a level keel and reminded me that, as Sir Thomas Beecham put it: 'There are two golden rules for an orchestra: start together and finish together'. This is not always as easy as it sounds!

Beating in differing time signatures

It is very useful to practise starting a piece at any point of a bar in any conventional time signature; one, two, three, four, five or six all have their different characteristics, and need individual repetition to feel – and look – effortless. A different issue, of course, arises with less conventional time signatures. The would-be conductor must be confident about beating five-time, either as 3+2 or 2+3 (and switching between them without anxiety). Yet more complex are multiple patterns such as eight (3+3+2 or 3+2+3) or eleven (which can come in a number of divisions). All of these can usefully be practised in front of a mirror and may well require quite a lot of attention. It is worth adding that the aspiring conductor should rehearse all these patterns with different dynamics. It is easier to beat multiple time signatures more economically than conventional patterns; it is still necessary to make a distinct difference between piano and forte.

There are countless books that provide diagrams of the shape of the beat for different time patterns. I do not intend to add to them. It is sensible to stick to a conventional shape as the alternatives may cause confusion to orchestral novices, but it is easy to over-estimate the importance of this. For example, when beating two beats in a bar, one would normally swing to the right on one and direct the second beat to the left as well as upwards. In practice, there are moments (particularly when you need to hold a pulse steady) when swinging towards the left and taking the upbeat upwards and to the right will be preferable. Conversely, an accelerando in two will work more smoothly if you use the conventional direction. This makes it easier to compress the second pulse of the bar as you move forward.

Sub-divisions of the pulse often cause anxiety. Generally speaking, the fewer beats you beat in any bar, the more helpful it will be; too much movement of the stick can create a slightly frantic impression. On the other hand, if the tempo becomes so slow that the beat no longer expresses a reliable forward pulsation, it will be difficult to follow or maintain. In particular, a final semiquaver at the end of the bar in a slow tempo may need the last beat of the bar divided into two quavers in order to produce an accurate ensemble. It is always sensible to try different degrees of sub-division at a rehearsal and let the ear tell you what is working best. If in doubt, ask your musicians which option they find more helpful.

The use of the left hand

The use of the left hand is another controversial question. What Boult described as the 'Grecian Urn' style, in which the two arms mirror each other, is manifestly both wasting conductorial energy and diluting the focus of the musicians. It is true that there are places where two hands in parallel can genuinely be helpful: the opening of the Finale of Brahms' Symphony No. 2, Op. 73, for example, somehow works better with a gentle gesture from both hands than with a small stick movement alone. Such a beginning is weakened with two preparatory beats – the obvious alternative to two hands – as surprise and the pianissimo dynamic both require the smallest movement possible to convey the magic implicit in the first few bars. This is an exception to the general rule, however, that the left hand should only convey something the right hand does not. It may be an issue of dynamic; the hand facing downwards implies a quieter sound, an open raised hand the opposite. The conductor can be far more subtle than that; tracing a line with a single finger can help the legato. A sharp movement with the left hand can assist unanimity with an accent, and diminuendo and crescendo can be maintained over an extended period, while a clear pulse is conveyed by the right hand. The left hand can also be used to indicate a lead to a player or singer – or a group. Such a gesture needs to be in enough time to enable the musician to breathe in advance and not to look patronising. These kinds of gesture do not need to be large; indeed, they scarcely need to be visible to the audience at all. Most communication of this kind is better done with the eye, but sometimes a small helpful hand movement can reduce any anxiety and enable the entry to be prompt and confident. There is a wonderful film on YouTube of Bernard Haitink conducting the Royal Concertgebouw Orchestra in Debussy's *La Mer*; in the last movement, he conducts a couple of cymbal strokes with the forefinger of the left hand. It is a miniature masterclass in how to time and scale a left-hand gesture and should be compulsory viewing for all who have an interest in conducting.

Directing solos

A regular point of discussion is the extent to which the conductor should direct recitative in Baroque music, and indeed, in any solo with an orchestra. I have seen a well-known conductor trying to conduct the flute player in the opening of Debussy's *Prélude à l'après midi d'un faune*; the player rightly disliked this impertinence – and overtly ignored the conductor until her solo was finished. The only question for the conductor to ask is, 'What is the most helpful thing I can do here?' If in doubt, ask the player what he or she would prefer. My own view, so far as recitative is concerned, is that I like to be in control of when the recitative starts and when it finishes; everything else is for the singer and the continuo partners to determine. Of course, when there is an attacca into a chorus, the conductor will need to beat any join between the two; such places are often potential mine fields, where clarity and an absence of histrionics will be the best way to ensure a secure performance.

Similar issues can arise when accompanying an operatic duet; do you let the singers resolve the final cadence and follow them, or do you direct it so that they are integrated into the final instrumental passage? The answer will normally depend upon the distance the singers are apart from each other, and the nature of the instrumental coda. An offbeat entry in the orchestra will probably mean that you need to conduct out of the previous bar, but even when it is simpler, some singers prefer a little left-hand direction to get their duet together if they are some distance apart. A very good work to study to demonstrate these dilemmas is Verdi's Requiem, where several of the solo passages need careful consideration regarding where to conduct and where to leave things entirely to the free choice of the soloists.

Instrumental soloists pose similar but not identical dilemmas. I discuss these in 'Orchestral Accompaniment' (see page 46), but as always, the best rule of thumb is to take the advice of your soloists regarding where they would like to be conducted, and where they would much prefer to be left alone in a dialogue with one or two orchestral soloists.

The ultimate test of any technique for any conductor is, 'Does this help to communicate the music?' A singer or instrumentalist has only to think of the audience. Uniquely, a conductor has to think both of the audience and of the ensemble being directed. This is the core of our task and the only real yardstick by which we may measure success and failure.

Preparation

In 1967 I moved to Surrey to become Director of Music at Cranleigh School. It was a big department with a tradition of music theatre performances, which included Mussorgsky's *Boris Godunov* as one of my early challenges. Tod Handley immediately involved me with the Guildford Philharmonic Orchestra (GPO) as his continuo player. The GPO was a part-time professional orchestra ('with amateur stiffening' in its early days, as Tod elegantly put it). Attending his rehearsals and concerts, and playing continuo when the repertoire required it, was deeply interesting and further increased my admiration for him as a conductor. In March 1968, I conducted a performance of Orff's *Carmina Burana* in Cranleigh, which I had to direct with my right leg in plaster after breaking an ankle skiing. In the audience were the Chairman and Secretary of the Guildford Choral Society. This led to an invitation to become Musical Director of this fine choir, which was in a slightly uncertain state following the abrupt departure of the previous conductor, David Taylor, to South Africa. It turned out to be the longest relationship of my life – forty years of productive and happy collaboration, which encompassed commissions and tours as well as performances of Britten's *War Requiem,* Elgar's *The Kingdom,* Walton's *Belshazzar's Feast* (three times) and a number of notable recordings.

Throughout this time, I was still regularly visiting Sir Adrian Boult to talk about scores. He would never accept any kind of payment, or even a present. Yet he must have given me dozens of hours of help and advice during my time in Surrey. Boult had a unique capacity to put his finger on a place where extra rehearsal would be necessary or where one would need to 'gather one's forces' with particular care.

Working with the Choral Society in Guildford gave me even more access to the Guildford Philharmonic Orchestra, with whom the choir sometimes collaborated, and to more of Tod Handley's rehearsals, to which I sometimes brought my sixth-form students. The GPO repertoire was extraordinary: one typical season included Bax, Delius, Lambert and Moeran, as well as an unforgettable performance of Stravinsky's *The Rite of Spring* and Bartók's Concerto for Orchestra. Tod's prodigious technique gave him a level of rhythmic control I have never seen equalled. His preparation was equally detailed; I do not remember seeing him ever make a gesture that did not simplify the task of his players, and though much of his repertoire was unusual, he always had a grasp both of the detail and the architecture of the music he was conducting. The only occasion he seemed less than comfortable was in a performance of Beethoven's 'Eroica' Symphony No. 3, Op. 55; with the ill luck that dogged much of his life, it was an occasion where Boult was in the audience. Tod seemed less relaxed and in command than usual and his head was more in the score than I had seen before. It may have been that his awareness of his mentor's presence had somehow put him on edge. Live performance takes no prisoners and can be both a source of stress and a source of excitement for the performers. It is one of the reasons why conducting requires a cool detachment as well as a passionate involvement in the music. This is not always an easy circle to square.

Memorising

The ability to memorise is at the heart of the conductor's role. The catchphrase 'The score in the head, not head in the score' should be a mantra for every conductor. It is not always easy to achieve this. Some musicians find memorisation straightforward: others do not. Listening to recordings, even when it is possible, is a mixed blessing. It can provide some shortcuts but internalising another conductor's interpretation has obvious dangers. More critically, it is important to learn not just the surface of the music, but what is underneath it as well. Conductors who use recordings as an aide memoire must be meticulous about listening to several different versions if that is possible. We all need to beware of taking on more new scores than we can really master in a given season; many fine young conductors have bitten off more than they can chew, and the orchestra always knows if a conductor's grip on the score lacks certainty. Carlo Maria Giulini, one of the finest Italian conductors of the post-war period, used to retreat to his Mediterranean island for at least a month when he had a new score to learn. For most of us, sadly, the imperative of earning a living makes this impossible. Many conductors have to learn scores under pressure but somehow, we have to create the necessary space in our diaries to ensure that new scores have time to 'settle in'.

I remember taking Elgar's *Enigma Variations* to Boult when I had first to conduct them in Guildford. I was finding the long accelerando in the final variation difficult to control and I asked him where he moved from three beats in a bar to one, as the music quickens. He replied, 'I go on several long country walks'. At the time, it seemed to me an unhelpful answer; with hindsight, it was clear that he meant that if I had to think about how many beats I was going to conduct at any point, I simply did not know the music well enough. That is a profound truth, and a good reason for not writing many instructions to yourself in the score. If you need to read them while conducting, you will be looking downwards more often than is helpful.

I have always found it useful to approach a new piece by reading it through at its real performance tempo. This enables one to see the peaks and troughs, the bigger and smaller climaxes scaled against each other and the moments of greatest intensity of emotion. It is also a useful way to spot passages that are going to be particularly difficult to play or sing. With a complex piece, most of us will certainly need to examine parts of the score in greater detail than merely reading through. It can be sensible to take the wind, strings and brass in separate blocks, and to rehearse a complex passage very slowly to make sure that the sounds are really being accurately imagined. Transposing instruments (which are written in a different key from the one in which they sound) are a further challenge for many conductors. It is often helpful to practise score-reading at the piano to assist with fluency in transposition and managing the less familiar C clef simultaneously with the more conventional treble and bass clefs.

Balance and tempo

Once the basic ingredients of the score are safely internalised, there will be a whole raft of musical issues to be resolved. Many of these are, of course, common to all performers. The one of orchestral balance, however, is specific to the conductor. Reading through the score, there will be places where you can see that the brass are going to be heavily in the foreground. To avoid nagging continuously at one's brass players, it is important to identify where in the score a saturation of brass sound will be thrilling, and where it will be destructive. A symphony by Mozart or Haydn will be less at risk from this than one by Berlioz or Tchaikovsky, but the conductor must seek to listen from the perspective of the audience. In earlier repertoire, there may well be a need to add some extra phrasing or dynamics to compensate for the limited information printed on the page. There were many conductors who 'improved' orchestrations of classical repertoire in the past. It is now done much more sparingly, and wisely so, but there are still one or two places – for example, the join between the third and fourth movements in Schumann's Symphony No. 4, Op. 120, where a little judicious thinning of the woodwind parts can help to achieve the pianissimo the composer requires.

As far as tempo is concerned, a conductor has the same challenges as any performing musician, compounded by issues of practicality. No sensible pianist will choose too fast a tempo that their fingers cannot sustain. It is all too easy for a conductor to select a tempo which feels great but which, in fact, requires more of the strings or woodwind than is really practical. On the other hand, there are quick passages that are actually harder to play slower with stringed ensembles because of the way that the bows move. On one occasion, I was conducting Glinka's *Ruslan and Lyudmila* overture with the BBC Concert Orchestra. I took what I thought was a helpfully moderate tempo, but the leader, John Bradbury (a very gifted violinist), said 'It would be a bit easier faster'. I was surprised, but he was quite right, and the performance was better for his advice. Consideration should also be given to wind players. There are tempi at which double tonguing is not possible on a wind instrument; there are also places where it is virtually impossible to play really quietly (the higher register of the flute, for example). All these issues should inform the preparation process.

When it comes to rubato, even the most technically gifted conductor has to allow for the fact that a large ensemble will respond, like a great ocean liner, a fraction slower than a small group. Conducting requires empathy for the difficulties faced by a player fifty feet away from you who is trying to play precisely together with a colleague on the other side of the orchestra. Helping a wind section to anticipate slightly is part of the conductor's job; ensuring that the bass line is not fractionally behind is another important task. In an orchestra – as in every musical ensemble – rhythm comes from the bass line, and no leader can compensate for a slightly erratic pulse underneath them. There is a memorable film of Arturo Toscanini abusing his bass players; very few conductors would want to talk to colleagues in that way.

This matter of basic pulse is the most crucial of all. Whatever tempo you have prepared for your overture or symphony may be subject to change in light of the hall, the players and even the weather. The crucial issue of 'the long country walks' you have taken to ensure that you really know the work will have given you a fundamental grasp but tempi cannot be cast in stone. Manifestly, you must allow for the resonance in your performance space to modify your tempi. Even in two good concert halls, a very quick tempo can be exhilarating in one and simply inarticulate in another. In a very resonant church – not necessarily designed for musical performance – it may be helpful to let the orchestra play a minute or two while you walk around the building to discover how the effects change in different parts of the space. Even in a very resonant space, that will not change the relationships *between* tempi, of course. As you develop your interpretation of a work, those relationships are more crucial than anything else.

As in all music, slow movements are likely to be harder than quicker ones in terms of pulse. Boult used to talk of 'swinging the beat over the bar line' in slow tempi; a skill that he had mastered to an exceptional degree. With a large ensemble in front of you, it is essential to provide a rhythmic pulsation that moves things forward *whatever the tempo*. Lightening the intermediate beats in a bar will be crucial for this but it will not be enough if you do not communicate a real sense of movement, even at adagio. I have always believed that the best test of a conductor is a slow movement by Mozart or Haydn where real musical judgment has to be demonstrated without the camouflage of rich texture or rhythmic complexity.

Preparation of orchestral parts

Preparing the orchestral parts is another important task for the conductor, particularly if rehearsal time is short. It may be difficult to do it if you do not have access to the material, or you have a librarian who is overstretched or is unwilling. If you have clearly decided bowings, it is always useful to get hold of the front string desks so that you can write in at least those in crucial moments. There are conductors who put in breathing marks in wind parts; I have never done this, as I prefer to leave judgments about these to experienced individual wind soloists. If you have the good fortune to have a permanent post with an orchestra, you will have must more access to the library and it is sensible to check the condition of the parts before you select a work for performance. The Wren Orchestra had a splendid library but I remember all too well trying to conduct Schubert's 'Unfinished' Symphony No. 8, D 759 from parts that were clearly approaching the end of their useful life. Such an apparently trivial difficulty can make players edgy; if a part can tear as you turn it over, that is an unlooked-for source of tension. A more entertaining distraction as a conductor is to find markings in your score from a previous performance by another conductor. This can sometimes be illuminating; on other occasions, they can raise serious doubts about a colleague's judgement. I conducted Mozart's 'Jupiter' Symphony No. 41, K. 551 several times in successive open-air concerts with the Wren Orchestra. Mosquitos are always a problem at these events and the score began increasingly to look more like a morgue for insects than a high musical achievement.

Editions

A final word about editions. A conductor can generally – but not always – specify the edition preferred. In any event, I strongly recommend not conducting from a different edition from the one you have used to prepare. Though one's musical memory is fundamentally aural, it can be very disconcerting to find a big moment on an unexpected side or part of the page, or even with rehearsal letters in unfamiliar places. This is a very good argument for checking editions carefully in plenty of time!

Programme Planning

The planning of programmes for public performance is one of the most fascinating tasks for a musician. Singers and instrumentalists share many issues with the conductor: the nature of the audience; the scale of the venue; the need to prioritise familiarity (to encourage an audience) while providing enough novelty to intrigue both musicians and audience. There is also the vital necessity of not overfilling the programme! (There is scope for a book on that one topic, but this is not that book.) There are, moreover, special considerations for conductors to confront as they construct programmes. Among those will be the danger of matching an over-filled rehearsal pattern to an over-filled concert. Further consideration will be needed over the resources – financial and technical – of the musicians whom you are going to direct, and the setting in which you are going to perform.

Financial considerations

Financial issues are all too relevant in most programme decisions, particularly in Britain, where funds are very seldom more than adequate, and very often less than that. If you are working with professional musicians, you will need carefully to consider the rehearsal implications of whatever programme you choose. You will not wish to have numbers of musicians sitting around while you rehearse another work with smaller forces. If you have, for example, an overture and a concerto that do not require trombones or percussion, try to call the extra players as late as possible if they only appear in the second half. In Brahms' symphonies, for example, instruments like the tuba or the contrabassoon may be used in some movements and not in others. The Brahms symphonies are particularly likely to waste players' time. If the trombones do not play in the first three movements, a thoughtful conductor will make a point of calling them later to the rehearsal so that they do not have to waste time sitting about backstage. With a programme of eight or nine short pieces, this of course, becomes more difficult to arrange but it is worth making a chart of the orchestrations of each piece to see how you can use your players' time in the least wasteful way possible. It is quite remarkable that some conductors will call for the full orchestra for a rehearsal and start by inviting half a dozen players to come back later; this does not help morale! A detailed rehearsal schedule needs to be prepared and circulated to the musicians in advance.

Specific issues arise with Baroque music, some of which may include an array of *obligato* instruments. Of course, the players will be booked and paid for a three-hour rehearsal but only the most insensitive conductor would want to have players sitting idly in the hall for an extended time. In a work like Handel's *Messiah* or one of Bach's Passions, the conductor must make a very detailed schedule which uses the musicians in the most time efficient way. Peter Hurford was brilliant at this; he would produce a schedule timed to within five minutes. This had the doubly beneficial effect of enabling players to know exactly when they were required and ensuring that he never lost control of the rehearsal.

Balancing familiar and less familiar repertoire

It is unwise to plan a programme of complicated modern music, even with the extraordinary flexibility of British orchestral players, if you only have a single rehearsal on the day. (This pattern is the model for more than half of the professional concerts given on these islands, a fact of which many audience members are blissfully unaware.) It would be a bold – or even a foolish – conductor who programmed an unknown piece of virtuosic writing on the basis of a single rehearsal. With my concerts for the splendid English Music Festival held annually in Dorchester Abbey, I very often found myself with quite a lot of unfamiliar repertoire (suggested to me by the indefatigable Em Marshall whose brainchild and success this excellent event has been). Invariably, we had a spirited debate in which I sought to balance some unknown – and often high-quality work – by composers such as Bliss, Dyson, Finzi, Howells or Rawsthorne, with more familiar material by Elgar, Holst or Vaughan Williams, so that not every piece challenged the players to the same degree in one evening. It is, moreover, very exhausting for players to have to play from handwritten parts throughout a three-hour rehearsal. Much neglected music has never been properly printed and the conductor should review the orchestral material to make sure that not too much is being asked of the players in this regard. The more unfamiliar the music, the more likely it will be that the parts contain mistakes, or at least, some illegibility. This will add stress to a three-hour rehearsal.

Of course, with more rehearsal time, the pressure may be less. Even so, unusual repertoire, whatever its artistic merit, may require a degree of editing at the rehearsal if the parts have had no recent use. Hired parts may also be of mixed quality; the parts for Walton's Symphony No. 1, for example, are notorious for having been written over by many generations of players. The last time I conducted the piece, it was challenging, not merely in its famous technical demands, but in the quality of eyesight required to make out the exact notes on the page.

A conductor is therefore wise to insist, so far as it is possible, on at least some extra overtime if there is only one preliminary rehearsal. There are practical ways in making this affordable. For example, if you have Rossini's *William Tell* overture programmed, try to obtain fifteen minutes overtime for the 'cello section so that the difficult opening can be tackled without the rest of the orchestra being paid to sit and listen to it. In the same way, Britten's *War Requiem* can be best rehearsed by overlapping the main and chamber orchestras in such a way that each rehearses for three hours while the conductor rehearses for four. This is exhausting but much less expensive than two full rehearsals. If you have one piece for strings only in the programme, try for half an hour's overtime to look at it before the other musicians arrive; this will reduce pressure without costing very much. Above all, do not lose control of the rehearsal schedule in a way that pushes you into unplanned overtime at the end of the rehearsal. This will not only cost your promoter extra money, but exasperate the players, the stewards and the piano tuner, if there happens to be one waiting.

Different considerations apply to youth orchestras, as discussed on page 57. With such a group, any sensible conductor is constantly watching to make sure that the young musicians are not overtiring themselves either physically or intellectually. The normal three-hour rehearsal limit for professional musicians generally works well; it is often inappropriate for younger players and singers.

Amateur and a cappella choirs

With amateur choirs, there are other problems to be confronted. Works like Stephen Oliver's *Prometheus* written in ancient Greek will tax any choir. The other works in the programme must take account of this. Tippett's *A Child of Our Time* is a wonderful work and choirs love the settings of the spirituals which punctuate the work and illuminate its message. The other choruses, however, though gripping for the audience (and it is, of course, a story with powerful resonances), are not so rewarding for the singers. I always try to find a vocally enjoyable work to pair with the Tippett so that the choir does not emerge from the concert wishing for 'a good sing'. Parry's *Blest Pair of Sirens* or Vaughan Williams' *Five Mystical Songs* provide a better pairing than, for example, Holst's *The Hymn of Jesus*, which is another fine work that singers find a bit of a struggle.

With an unaccompanied choir, things are simultaneously simpler and more challenging. Because the choir will be singing continuously, concentration will generally (if the choir is properly trained!) be easier to maintain than in a work with extensive solo and/or orchestral passages during which the choir has nothing to do. On the other hand, if some singers begin to become fatigued before the end of the concert, with a consequent diminution in either pitch or quality of tone, you have nowhere to hide. One of the unique challenges of a choral conductor in such circumstances is to find gestures and facial expressions that can help to reinvigorate a choral group for the final section of the concert. There are particular works which are unusually daunting. Tallis' *Spem in alium nunquam habui* is a case in point. Though not intrinsically difficult to pitch, it is very difficult for a singer to find their place if they become detached from the tutti. I always insist in this piece that we have one or two places which can be recognised as 'gathering points'. Thankfully, I have never had to deploy these in a concert but I have rehearsed 'emergency procedures' at rehearsal – not always with immediate success! Vaughan Williams' Mass in G Minor, surely one of his greatest conceptions, requires a choir to have a deeply secure sense of pitch. An equally challenging work following it would be a misjudgement; you need to find something stylistically comparable but less demanding in terms of intonation.

When attending to the question of resources, a choral conductor must obviously be mindful of the choir's strengths and weaknesses. If your tenor section is slightly less convincing than the others, avoid a divided tenor part. If your sopranos are young and mellifluous, it is sensible to programme to that strength rather than inviting them to sing rather strident middle European music where sheer volume is a crucial factor in the dynamic range required.

Amateur orchestras

If you are conducting an amateur orchestra, develop a policy with your Chairman and Treasurer to deal with buying in professional players to 'stiffen' your ensemble and cover any missing instruments. Budgeting for this is part of the conductor's role and nothing creates tension more surely than to confront the Treasurer with an additional demand to pay the cost of a harpist, a contrabassoonist or a vibraphone player at the last minute. Common sense should dictate that if you are going to bring in additional players beyond the usual, you should try to ensure that they do not play only for a few minutes in a concert. This is unsatisfying for them and not cost-effective for the orchestra. I am often surprised by how frequently a conductor appears to be unaware of one or two unusual instruments which have been implicitly demanded by programming a particular piece.

Consider your audience

We all need to empathise with our audience. Some of them will be enthusiasts who know much of the repertoire well. Others – conceivably a majority – will be hearing much of the music for the first time. The performers have the map in front of them with 'the journey' written out in musical notation. The audience do not have this advantage; they may have no idea whether the piece is twenty minutes long or double that. The quality of the programme notes may or may not help in this regard and in any event, often are not read until after the concert is over. This leads me to suggest that we should be cautious when constructing programmes more than ninety minutes long. Of course, many operas occupy more than three hours but the action on the stage adds something that no conventional concert can provide. The experience of the audience should be at the front of the conductor's mind both in the planning and the execution of every concert. Our job is to help people to enjoy and be engaged by great music. If we offer too much material in one evening, we may not succeed in this key task. (For more on this see 'The Conductor and the Audience', page 80.)

Instrumentation

I have one final thought for the conductor working on a programme. If you are listing a piece that you do not know well, do not rely upon the various catalogues to give you the exact instrumentation. There are many inaccuracies in catalogues and it is a foolish conductor who programmes a work without having seen the complete full score, ascertained the availability of parts and read through the piece to assess its difficulty. A couple of specific examples will suffice. The orchestration of Haydn's *Nelson Mass* calls for three trumpets. In fact, never more than two are essential. The third trumpet adds something exciting and dramatic in the 'Benedictus' but it is entirely possible to do without it, if funds are restricted. It is not, on the other hand, practical to perform Dvořák's Symphony No. 8, Op. 88, without a cor anglais. Walton's *Belshazzar's Feast* can be performed without the offstage bands (though something significant is lost) but to omit instruments from Britten's

War Requiem would change the sound world of the piece in a destructive way. Vaughan Williams' *A Sea Symphony* and Holst's *Hymn of Jesus* have a number of instruments that can be dispensed with; the composers happily offer the conductor a priority list to indicate in which order instruments may be omitted. One learns what works – or does not – by experience. If a piece is new to you, look at it carefully before you commit to its rehearsal and performance.

Performance and Presentation

Prepare for the unexpected

Sitting in the dressing room waiting for the concert to begin is the moment of greatest responsibility for the conductor, however well you may have rehearsed, because the unexpected can come upon you at any time. The list of challenges I have known could fill an entire book on their own, but I remember two or three particularly perilous events. On one occasion, the wonderful 'cellist, Rohan de Saram, broke a string at the beginning of the slow movement of Dvořák's Cello Concerto, Op. 104; he had to leave the stage to install a new string and I had to distract the audience with an anecdote which kept them engaged without adding a too frivolous note to the wonderful atmosphere Rohan had achieved before his string snapped. He returned and played magisterially, though he had to retune before the final movement and both of us were preoccupied by concerns over intonation.

Choral staging always carries an element of risk; on another occasion, somehow a bass singer managed to fall off the back row in the final section of a performance of Walton's *Belshazzar's Feast*. I decided to keep going, and luckily, two of the hapless singer's colleagues elegantly extracted themselves from the choir and ensured that no serious medical problem had occurred. In a previous performance of *Belshazzar's Feast*, I was conducting a very large choir; to ensure that I was visible, the podium was unusually high and the music stand at full stretch. Two minutes before the end (which has multiple changes of metre), the stand slowly descended to its minimum height well beyond my field of vision. Fortunately, my memory was just good enough to get through to the end but my final gestures were histrionic with relief. Minor difficulties like the baton disengaging itself from the conductor's hand, or simply breaking in the middle of a bar, simply require the conductor to keep calm and carry on. It is more complicated if lights fail, or, as in one northern concert hall, simply go dark. These kind of emergencies will test the grace of a conductor but they are all part of the responsibility we accept by climbing onto the podium.

Things do not always work out so well; Vernon Handley had a retina detach in the middle of a concert. He lost his balance as a consequence. Bravely, but I think mistakenly, he called for a stool and finished the concert before going to hospital. This was a magnificent example of 'the show must go on', but the loss of sight that resulted was too a high a price to pay for his duty to the audience. Conductors can be taken less seriously ill in performance: I once observed a famous conductor leave the stage two minutes before the end of a Mahler symphony in order vomit into a fire bucket at the side of the stage. This could have been a marvellous opportunity for an assistant, or even a student in the audience but in fact, the orchestra finished the symphony perfectly well without the conductor.

Generally speaking, 'Doctor Stage' comes to your aid. We conductors are often required to perform with a cold or a fever; adrenaline normally shuts down the symptoms for the duration of the concert. In any circumstance, however, the conductor has to make the ultimate decision about whether to continue or interrupt a performance. This is not always clear cut. For example, if you have an organ which 'ciphers' (or plays by itself!), you would obviously stop if it were loud. On the other hand, if it is just a drone, you might press on in the hope, either that the organist will turn the instrument off, or that the cipher will resolve itself. (If you are beating alternate bars of 3 and 4 at the same time as considering this question, a cool head is required!)

Dealing with nerves and other practical matters

All performers have some sense of nervousness before going onto the platform. I have always advised my students to focus on the music they are about to conduct to distract them from nerves; the only real measure of a good performance is that the audience are delighted with the music. Sir Adrian Boult, who always looked magisterially calm, was in fact in a state of high tension before performances. If he arrived too early to the dressing room, he would often go for a walk to settle his nerves; audience members were sometimes nonplussed to see him walking away from the hall half an hour before the concert was scheduled to begin! Boult always used to say that he would prefer to have the conductor behind a screen so that there was nothing to distract the audience from the *sound* of the music. The modern focus on 'personality' does not encourage this, but the conductor is never more important than the composer at any stage. When things have apparently gone very well, it is always crucial for us to remember that key point.

How best to prepare physically for a performance is an interesting question. The issue of whether to eat before a concert, and if so, how much, is much less trivial than it initially sounds. Indigestion is an unhelpful accompaniment to conducting but most people's energy will diminish if they have fasted before a show. Slow-energy-release foods as taken by athletes – bananas for example – are good choices; alcohol, almost always, an unwise one. Conductors' dressing rooms are often not ideal places to lurk in for an hour or more before the event; I rather prefer a short walk in the open air if it is possible, although you may occasionally get alarmed looks from audience members if they see you walking away from the hall before the concert is due to start.

Clothing can provide anxious moments. On one occasion, I arrived at the hall in Milton Keynes to conduct with my normal suit carrier, only to discover, when I came to change after the rehearsal, that the trousers had somehow absented themselves. Luckily, the piano soloist was a close male friend of mine. I donned his trousers for the overture (Beethoven's *Fidelio*), changed into the fourth horn's trousers for Saint-Saëns' Piano Concerto No. 2, Op. 22 (which only employed two horn players), and during the interval, was able to borrow the trousers of a board member of similar height to myself who had kindly gone home in the first half to collect them. Ever since, I check both the wardrobe arrangements and the scores I need with me at least twice before departure.

Forgetting to bring the required scores is indeed another potential source of anxiety. One broadcast of a new work was famously aborted when the conductor, who had taken the band parts home to insert some markings, left the entire set on the train. I always ask the orchestral librarian to provide a score, even if I have one of my own, so that there is a little cover. Of course, if it is a new work, there may be only one score so extra care is clearly required.

A wise conductor will reconnoitre the access route to the rostrum through the orchestra, in good time. It can be very tight on some stages and knocking a music stand over can be a most unhelpful start to a concert. I try to avoid having to negotiate an obstacle course on the way to my place; it adds to tension just when calm is required. Some deep breaths before you enter the hall will help to keep the pulse rate at a reasonable level; a smile for the audience, as long as it is not too self-conscious, provides an impression of goodwill which generally gets things off to a good start. A smile for your performers is no bad thing either; they have to do most of the work for you – it is helpful to make clear that you are aware of that and grateful for their support. Before the first upbeat, try to stand absolutely still, to look your players in the face with an expression appropriate to the mood of the opening bars and enjoy the growing silence from the audience as they wait for you to commence. If you wait too long, the audience may start to cough and the 'atmosphere' and concentration can dissipate. Experience teaches one to have a clear idea of this crucial hiatus, but it is probably better to start too soon rather than to wait too long.

It is very important to make sure that all your players are ready. I remember starting the last movement of J. S. Bach's Double Violin Concerto BWV 1043 having failed to spot that the two violinists had taken their instruments off their chins to tune. The result was embarrassing; I always take a panoramic look round the orchestra now before I give the upbeat.

The conductor's role in a concert

The conductor's role in a concert is wholly different from that in the rehearsal. In rehearsal, you should be analysing what you hear, considering what can be improved and what gestures will demonstrate how you want a similar passage to be played next time it appears. In the performance, your task is to help your players feel absolutely confident about how and when to play what the composer has written. There is no need to give leads to those who do not need them – that just looks patronising and self-important – but there is every need to give assistance to a player who may find a particular entry slightly problematic. Give too much help rather than too little, but as inconspicuously as possible. There are places in many famous works where it is genuinely difficult for the players to be absolutely together; you must know where these are and prepare to gather your forces well in advance of those particular moments. Many of these places will involve changes of tempo: the gear change at the end of Dvořák's Symphony No. 8, Op. 88, or the accelerando into the Coda of Brahms' Symphony No. 1, Op. 68, for example. There are other places, however, such as the point when the three tunes combine in Wagner's *Die Meistersinger von Nürnberg* prelude, where the tempo can wobble unless you are absolutely clear and looking directly at the players.

There are issues of tempo also, not only for the music itself, but for the concert. The gap between movements or sections is not laid down by the composer beyond the occasional *lunga pausa* mark at the end of a movement, yet it is manifestly wrong to move to a rapid *attacca* after a slow movement has gently died away in a riveting pianissimo. Equally, there are many places (between the third and fourth movements of Tchaikovsky's Symphony No. 4, Op. 36, for example) where a delay destroys the excitement and surprise of the drama. I tend to err on the side of shorter rather than longer breaks between sections; we need to remember that the audience has generally less knowledge and less commitment to the music than we have and we should try to help them hold their concentration for as long as they can. For this reason, I also dislike leaving the platform between items unless I am going to fetch a soloist or a number of players are leaving or joining the platform. Some of my colleagues seem to enjoy a leisurely space between items but I do notice that the audience quite often begins to move around in their seat if too much delay is allowed. I watched Reginald Smith Brindle – an esteemed conductor of new music – remove a large spotted handkerchief from his pocket and blow his nose noisily upon it between sections of a very sparsely-orchestrated twelve-note work in the Royal Albert Hall. For some of us it was the high point of the piece, but I do not think he helped either the composer or the audience by that hiatus. In Classical repertoire, I am equally dismayed when a conductor cuts an exposition repeat from a symphonic first movement to save time and then allows a couple of minutes to elapse before starting the second.

At the end of the concert, it is crucial to remember to acknowledge your musicians in a way that clearly conveys to the audience the true partnership between you and them. In particular, to acknowledge an orchestral soloist who has provided a particularly beautiful solo passage is essential. It may be helpful to write a list on an insert inside the back page of the score to remind oneself of those players who are likely to have earned extra appreciation. In the mixture of fatigue, delight and relief that characterises this moment, it is easy to forget to share the applause. All of us need acknowledgement if we do something well; it is the conductor's job to act as 'manager' in this context, and not to seek to bask in the audience's approbation when their contribution would have been non-existent without the musicians in front of them.

Rehearsals

Rehearsals come in many shapes and sizes. You may have a whole week with a youth orchestra on a residential course, nine consecutive weekly rehearsals with an amateur choir or orchestra, or a single three-hour rehearsal on the day of the concert with a professional British orchestra (in Europe or America it would be most unlikely to be asked to prepare a concert with so little rehearsal time, but it is quite usual in Britain). Each provides a different challenge, of course, but all call for meticulous planning, combined with the ability to flex your plan if things do not work out as you expect.

How to begin

With professional groups it is generally better to begin with a fairly substantial amount of music-making. Nothing is more dispiriting for orchestral players than to be stopped as soon as they have started in a rehearsal. All musicians need a bit of time to adjust to the room, to one another, and to the task in hand. The conductor's first duty is to radiate enthusiasm for the music and goodwill for his colleagues, not to give a lecture. Professional musicians are, in any case, suspicious of conductors with an overly academic approach; giving experienced musicians instruction in the nature of the music they are going to rehearse is likely to be counter-productive. 'Less is more' is a useful motto for most conductors when dealing with professional musicians.

With amateur and youth groups it is slightly different. An amateur choir will need to warm up; it is not helpful and can be damaging for their voices to be used too intensively too soon in the rehearsal. Equally important is the obvious truth that many of them will have come in a hurry from work or home to get to the rehearsal. Five minutes of inspiring introduction either to the music or to the goals of the rehearsal may well be useful in order to settle them down and focus their attention on the work in hand. Even so, conductors can easily overuse their own voices when what is needed is clear direction and a sense of a plan being followed. This is more likely to help the singers to do their best work.

It is worth mentioning another point about amateur choirs. A physically taxing piece; for example, Beethoven's Symphony No. 9, Op. 125, or Bach's B Minor Mass, may stress your singers – particularly the sopranos and tenors – at rehearsal. If you have a skilled accompanist, it is definitely worth rehearsing these pieces down a semitone until a week or two before the concert. Of course, singers with perfect pitch will not like it, but if you give your choir time to have learned the music comfortably, it is then much easier to focus on technique to ensure that the top of the voice is being used wisely without worrying about accuracy of detail.

The pace of work

I have always found it wise to do the most intense and detailed work just before the half-time break in the rehearsal. The prospect of refreshment (a most desirable feature of any rehearsal!) sustains an ensemble's attention. Towards the end of the rehearsal, when people are tiring, is not the best time for taking something to pieces, nor keeping some musicians waiting while others rehearse. We conductors need to remind ourselves that, however intense our concentration, we are almost certainly using less physical energy than those we are conducting. Having a couple of minutes to relax is often helpful and any good manager knows that this can appear spontaneous, even if it has been planned. Those two minutes can be the moment for the conductor to talk about some aspect of the performance that requires special focus, or even the telling of a joke (if you are confident that it will be amusing!).

Sometimes in a rehearsal, things will go badly. Occasionally there may be colleagues who are struggling; sometimes there will be those who clearly find you uncongenial or irritating. It is very unlikely to be helpful to take refuge either in sarcasm or aggression in such circumstances. Certainly, to allow oneself to lose one's temper is generally a mistake; you can scarcely expect to control other people if you cannot control yourself. Sir Adrian Boult did sometimes lose his self-control in rehearsals, though I think he always regretted it afterwards. He could be very frightening and this did sometimes challenge the players' deep respect for him in a way that seemed to me unproductive. On the other hand, all conductors have to be capable of exerting authority when there is either apathy or carelessness creeping into a rehearsal. It is wise to try to diffuse a sense of tension with a moment of gentle self-deprecation, simultaneously raising the energy level so as to reduce the opportunity for any kind of disruption. Of course, there may be sources of tension other than the conductor, much as paranoia or self-regard may persuade us otherwise! A full-time orchestra is a close-knit social group. Sexual entanglements, personal tragedies or even vendettas can – and do – occur. You may not learn of this at the time so it is sensible to assume that tension in the rehearsal room may have more than one cause. Like any manager, the conductor's best course is to try to create a congenial and mutually respectful atmosphere and let people get on with their work as well as they can.

The pace of the rehearsal is crucial; if it is too slow, the players will become bored and focus will be lost. It is fatuous to enquire if people are ready to play after you've made some musical or technical point. Your eyes should provide the answer to that question without the need for it to be asked. A sense of purpose requires quite a brisk pace in rehearsal. It is, however, possible to talk too fast and to leave people behind, particularly if you are rehearsing in a resonant acoustic. Maintaining eye contact with the musicians at the back of the ensemble, whether singers or players, is absolutely vital. This applies whether you are conducting or speaking.

It is important, whatever the length of the rehearsal period, that you maintain a sense of growing momentum that delivers the performers to the performance at the peak of preparation. It is a little like making a soufflé (or so I am told): if you peak too soon it is as unhelpful as if you are not ready in time. Certainly, the candlepower delivered in the performance must be higher than at any time in the rehearsal process; to get a brilliant sound in a rehearsal is only useful if you can reproduce it in the concert.

Another danger of rehearsing at too high an intensity is that it is very easy for singers to use too much voice at a rehearsal on the day of the concert; brass and wind players too can put their lips under pressure by over-doing it in the afternoon. I remember one very distinguished trumpeter becoming visibly stressed by the pressure on his lip, having played all the way through Walton's *Belshazzar's Feast* twice in one day. With greater experience, I would have insisted that he left out one or two passages in the rehearsal, to enable him to give a hundred per cent throughout the concert without undue stress. Most solo singers are very good at 'marking' at the rehearsal; some are almost too good at it and are reluctant to let the orchestra hear the true balance at any time before the concert. This can have its own dangers because the conductor needs to know exactly how much or little orchestral sound will be a true balance when the soloist is in full voice. I always encourage my soloists to sing out once or twice in the rehearsal and to spend the rest giving as much or as little as they prefer.

Practical considerations

Sometimes one has to rehearse in a different room from the venue of the concert. For amateur musicians this is an almost universal issue; some rehearsal rooms can be problematic. I have, even with professional players, had to rehearse in a room that is on a single level, where they had great difficulty in hearing each other. (I recall several Christmas concerts at London's Royal Albert Hall (RAH), when the final rehearsal was in Baden Powell House down the road, as an afternoon concert was taking place at the RAH. We would all arrive through the famous Bull Run entrance at 6.20 p.m. for a ten-minute seating rehearsal; the next time we came onto the platform would be for the concert!)

Another potential problem is lighting. It is important to avoid conducting in front of a window or with a strong light behind you; being dazzled as you look at the conductor is a powerful disincentive for doing so! Very harsh strip lighting, for example, is intrinsically tiring for both musicians and conductor. Ventilation is yet another issue: air conditioning can make rooms very cold; bad insulation create hot-houses in high summer. Both make concentration hard and the conductor should be both aware and sympathetic in these conditions. You cannot, unfortunately, change the shape or the room or become a lighting or heating engineer. Some players will expect the conductor to deal with these sorts of issues which are clearly beyond his or her control or any reasonable expectation. I have occasionally had to point this out! Orchestral and stage managers have a curious habit of absenting themselves from rehearsals just when they are needed to talk to a technician or stage hand to make some modification to enable the singers or players to feel comfortable. (One BBC orchestra was notorious for disliking a particular studio; one could almost predict the point at which two or three players would begin to complain about the air conditioning.)

Staging is another potential source of difficulty; not every stage manager understands fundamental truths such as the need for string players to have room to move their bow arms comfortably or the legitimate desire of back desk violas or 'celli not to be directly in front of a trombone or trumpet section. There is an increasing understanding that orchestral players' hearing can be damaged by excessive high sound levels day after day in rehearsals. Not all theatres, however, can supply protective screens; the conductor should always encourage orchestras to restrain their fortes in rehearsal to help to protect the general wellbeing of colleagues.

Open-air concerts present yet another set of challenges. Most al fresco performance spaces have a decent stage and it is normally covered. But rain can sometimes be blown onto the front of the stage; I remember conducting Constant Lambert's *Rio Grande* with the ebullient pianist, Anthony Goldstone, when his right sleeve became so sodden with rainwater that he could barely lift his arm off the keyboard! At the other extreme, if the sun shines fiercely onto the stage during an afternoon rehearsal, string players will become justifiably agitated by the possibility of damage to their instruments; glue melts! I have known occasions when this forced an extended break because no player will risk an expensive instrument in order to reassure the conductor that the ensemble will be convincing in the performance.

Another decision for the conductor to make is whether to stand or sit in a rehearsal. If you want to sit, a high stool is certainly necessary; standing is probably better but it is tiring to do so for two or three hours and it may be that fatigue will dilute your capacity to be inspiring, energetic and enthusiastic. If you decide to sit it is worth ensuring that someone will provide you with a stool if you are going to a venue with which you are unfamiliar. For many years I carried a stool in the back of my car when driving to concerts, just in case. (About a decade ago, I allowed a particular charming double-bass player to exchange my rather good stool for their less good one; in hindsight, this was definitely taking collegiality too far!) It is worthwhile to consider here the issue of the height of the podium upon which you are going to stand. There is no virtue in being elevated if all the players can see you perfectly well as you stand on the platform in front of them. If you have climbed onto a platform a metre above the level of the main platform, your front desk players will be looking at your knees unless they jerk their heads upwards whenever they need to see the beat. The leading desks, upon whom you are relying most intensively, will have a particularly gloomy time straining their necks to see you. You do not add to your authority by standing on top of two or three boxes. With a large choir, you may need a little more height but there are obvious risks attached to extending the music stand too high. With amateur choirs, you may find the rehearsal room to be manifestly inadequate and equipped with a piano that is far from an ideal standard. You may occasionally be confronted with an electronic keyboard which will have a deadening effect on your rehearsal. It is important that tricky passages are taught by 'call and response'. A difficult phrase should be demonstrated by voice or piano and then repeated by the choir. Having the pianist play vocal parts over the singers can develop a dangerous dependency; singers will need to have the sounds in their heads before performing them. A mixed ability choir will find it difficult to watch the conductor in the early stages of rehearsal. It is sensible to have a 'heads down, heads up' system with the singers, which ensures that they understand the importance of the latter! With less experienced singers, it may well be better for the conductor to play the piano (assuming a reasonable level of keyboard technique) with the singers around the piano (if practical), so that the echoing of particular passages can take place without having to be relayed to an accompanist first. With an extended rehearsal schedule, such as most amateur choirs require, planning will be a key ingredient. You may well wish to disseminate a rehearsal schedule so that if a singer misses a rehearsal, he or she knows what was covered and can do some homework. Each of the rehearsals needs to include new work and recapitulation of previous weeks. You will aim to be able to spend the final couple of rehearsals singing extended passages and needing to correct only a small number of uncertainties. Orchestral conducting brings with it the particular problem of establishing a bowing style with the string section. I always try to obtain 30-minutes' overtime with the strings before the tutti rehearsal so that the leader and I can get some basic stylistic questions settled without requiring wind and brass to sit doing nothing while we do so. If at all possible, the conductor should use string parts that have already been bowed; of course, you can change particular passages, but at least, you will not have to start with a virgin page of notes, the bowing of which can take up valuable time. Most leaders understand the need for haste in this matter. However, I have occasionally met leaders who want to discuss the bowing of individual bars at considerable length when time is already scarce. You will require tact and finesse to move things on at a brisk pace without appearing not to care about the bowing, which is, of course, a key factor in the sound your orchestra will produce. Other leaders can be brilliant at writing in bowings at high speed. John Ludlow, who led my first concert with the London Mozart Players and the Guildford Philharmonic Orchestra on many occasions, could write bowings into a part at an astonishing speed. This is a huge bonus for the conductor.

The conductor should make every effort to know the names of the players. It is wise to ask for a list in advance and to try to memorise it before you meet your colleagues. There is something unsatisfactory about addressing someone as 'Oboe' or 'First Trombone'. Some of us are better than others at memorising names – I am particularly bad at it – but it is a matter of basic courtesy and the players will prefer it if you recognise them by name. Clearly, it will be easier to memorise names of an amateur group that you see on a regular basis but if you have 180 singers in front of you, names may be difficult even after many months of rehearsals. I formed the habit when conducting youth orchestras of calling all the boys 'John' and all the girls 'Mavis' and invited them to contradict that greeting with their real name if they wished. Most young players found it amusing; Ben Glassberg, now one of our leading young conductors, was principal timpanist in the National Children's Orchestra. He took to calling his percussion section in the NCO 'John' and 'Mavis' which seemed not to ruffle any feathers, but I would not recommend it with any professional ensemble! Malcolm Sargent was inclined in his later career to address young male players as 'boy'. This did not endear him to orchestras. The first flute in my orchestra in Milton Keynes, Graham Mayger, had been principal piccolo in the BBC Symphony Orchestra in his early twenties. Many years after encountering Sargent, he was still seething about the way he had been treated.

Rehearsal tempi and acoustics

Rehearsal tempi are an interesting issue. In the early stages of rehearsal, one might well rehearse under the final tempo to enable the players or singers to have a little more time to see the notes. On the other hand, it is a mistake to allow the tempi in the performance – particularly the quicker ones – to become markedly more breathless than during any rehearsal. There are conductors who drive everything to the very limit of practicability, indeed, sometimes well past it, but this seems to me deeply unlikely to fulfil the composer's intentions. A quick tempo that is slightly too fast is as boring as a slow tempo that lacks momentum. It is often forgotten that contrapuntal music needs a little more time to register with the audience than lighter-textured pieces; in Wagner's *Die Meistersinger von Nürnberg* overture, for example, the combination of the three tunes has to have enough time to breathe if the listeners are to appreciate the full grandeur of the conception.

I have already laid stress on the need to differentiate between rehearsal and performance. The same understatement at rehearsal applies equally to conductors as it does to all the forces before them. It is sensible not to beat every bar in a rehearsal unless it is actually necessary. You will focus your performers better if you stop from time to time, 'step back' and listen to exactly what is emerging. Particularly in a strange hall, why not leave the platform and spend two or three minutes anticipating what the audience will experience? It is always dangerous to assume that what you hear on the rostrum is what the audience is also hearing. In some halls, balances change markedly as you go further from the platform; in some rooms – especially churches – the resonance is such that you may need to shorten many notes to achieve coherence for the listener. All these things have to be dealt with at pace in most circumstances, so it is wise to build in a little contingency time to your rehearsal plan for off-rostrum peregrinations! In 1985 I conducted two performances on consecutive days of Wagner's *Siegfried Idyll* with the orchestra of the Birmingham School of Music (now the Royal Birmingham Conservatoire). The first, in the lovely Adrian Boult Hall, went splendidly; the second, in the dead acoustic of Sutton Coldfield Town Hall, was sadly unsuccessful. I had failed to invite the players to lengthen all the staccatos – particularly those over-length notes – and with a full audience, it sounded as though every chord had ended prematurely. That was clearly my failure, not the orchestra's; it reminded me of the need to think of the listener's experience at every stage of every rehearsal – even if you have played the repertoire successfully on a previous occasion.

Rehearsing with soloists

Rehearsing with soloists is another absorbing issue. In many choral concerts, the vocal soloists will appear on the day of the concert at the orchestral rehearsal and sing together for the first time. If they are good musicians, they will almost certainly give a perfectly decent performance, but careful balancing of a quartet or nuances of shape that you have spent weeks teaching the choir will probably be unachievable. Even issues of pronunciation may be controversial; there is nothing worse than trying to agree the pronunciation of 'excelsis' (as in 'cello', or as in 'shell', or even as in 'cell'?) while the choir and orchestra sit and do nothing. Far better to have had a piano rehearsal with your vocal soloists on a previous day and to have ironed out these matters before you are anywhere near the orchestra. I have dealt elsewhere (see 'Orchestral Accompaniment', page 46) with the question of instrumental soloists; it is less usual to meet them for the first time on the day of a concert and one should try hard to avoid that.

Dealing with the unexpected

If you have planned your rehearsal(s) carefully, both you and your performers should be able to enter the auditorium for the concert with an assumption that all will go smoothly. Some performances generate fantastic electricity, some merely a quiet satisfaction, but if the preparation has been properly achieved, you should never have to leave the stage feeling that you have let the composer down. We can face unpredictable problems, of course. One of the best examples of this was when Meredith Davies conducted both Holst's *The Planets* and his *Hymn of Jesus* in Thaxted Church (where Holst founded a festival) with the Philharmonia and a massed choir. My Holst Singers had been engaged to provide the female semi-chorus for both pieces; I was there with the rather light, but enjoyable task, of directing the singers offstage for *The Planets*. It was an ambitious programme to rehearse in two hours and forty minutes, but Meredith was completely in command and had clearly planned everything meticulously. After twenty minutes, a policeman appeared, announcing that all cars parked outside the church must be moved. More than thirty players stood up and made for the exit. It was too early to call a break, so some twenty minutes were gratuitously lost without warning while the players found alternative parking spaces. It was an object lesson for me to observe how Meredith quietly accelerated the rehearsal tempo so that he had still played every note in the programme by two minutes before the scheduled end. He averted both the danger of running overtime or of music being played for the first time at the concert. It taught me that conductors need to be ready to contend with the unexpected which no planning – however detailed – can anticipate.

An interesting question is the extent to which you allow guests at rehearsals. Boult was extremely generous in this regard; he allowed his students, ex-students and other acquaintances to attend rehearsals. His secretary, Mrs Beckett, would regularly send out a couple of dozen rehearsal passes. Holst, who was an early recipient of one of these, described the attendees as 'the BMB (Bother Mrs Beckett) Club'. It would be more complicated to establish such a group nowadays. Issues of security have made halls more cautious about admitting visitors and there maybe safeguarding issues for younger attendees. That said, I think it is very informative for people to observe the rehearsal process and I have always tried to be welcoming to visitors at rehearsals. The Royal Philharmonic Orchestra (RPO) has developed very good community relations in many of the towns and cities to which it goes to play. Quite often, a group of children who have been involved in musical workshops as part of the RPO's outreach programme have come to a rehearsal; I have always enjoyed this and tried to make time to say a few words to them about the music we are rehearsing. Some of my colleagues refuse to rehearse at all if they can see a single figure in the hall. During my Oxford days, I spent a couple of months in America playing the organ and attending such orchestral rehearsals as I could access. When in Philadelphia for a week, I made the acquaintance of one of the violinists in the famous orchestra. He promised to get me into one of Eugene Ormandy's rehearsals. I was thrilled, of course. Arriving at the hall ten minutes before the rehearsal, I was admitted by a doorman who had early been briefed by my new friend. I went into the hall and sat somewhere I thought would be inconspicuous. At 10 a.m., Ormandy arrived. He looked round the hall before he began rehearsing and our eyes met briefly. I thought nothing of this; he turned round and began to rehearse. Ten minutes later, he put down the stick in apparent irritation and said in a loud voice, 'I sense a stranger in the hall; they must leave at once.' Embarrassed and upset, I shuffled away but I do not think that I ever bought a disk of Ormandy's after that! Fifty-five years later, I still feel saddened by this conductorial posturing. I cannot see an advantage in a tradition of secrecy where orchestral rehearsals are concerned, though obviously, listeners must not distract from the work in hand.

Orchestral layout

There is a final matter that the conductor must consider before his first rehearsal. This is the vexed question of orchestral layout. Before the twentieth century, the general principle was that first violins were seated on the conductor's left and second violins on the conductor's right. The violas and 'cellos were then placed in front of him. Behind them would be the flutes and oboes with the clarinets and bassoons behind them, in order that they could all hear each other very easily to facilitate tuning – a particularly crucial issue for woodwind players. In the twentieth century, the majority of conductors have preferred to have both violin sections on their left. The 'cellos are then generally placed on the right with the basses in a line behind them. This layout undeniably makes ensemble between first and second violins easier; most violinists prefer it. On the other hand, there is something unsatisfactory about having all the treble sound on one side and all the bass sound on the other. Particularly, in the music of the Classical period, it weakens the dialogue between first and second violins which is so often a feature of the texture of that style. Moreover, it tends to make the second violins less prominent to the audience's ears – a particular problem with 'linear' composers like Brahms and Wagner. Listening to Boult's performance of Wagner's *Die Meistersinger* overture, one heard a richer soundscape as the counterpoint between the two violin sections weaved around each other. (This may have been partly because one could actually see the second violins playing their contrapuntal entries.)

I have still not entirely resolved this issue in my mind. With the London Mozart Players, who have a particular affinity with the Classical style, I almost always place the second violins on my right. With larger symphony orchestras, however, I sometimes revert to the more conventional layout. Both versions, and indeed, a third which places the violas on the conductor's right, have their advocates in Europe and it is a matter which probably cannot be resolved. In a one-rehearsal concert, such as we have to contend with all too often in the UK, it may be wise to accept an orchestra's usual layout. When I have more than one rehearsal, I tend to insist on the second violins on my right – and I try hard to woo the principal second violin into relishing the challenge!

The positioning of the violins represents the most difficult decision for a conductor but there are other important choices to be made. Some of these will be dictated by the size and shape of a platform, of course, but if you have a spacious stage and freedom of choice, you will need to think about a number of factors. The timpani (and percussion) are often parked on one side of the stage at the back. There is no doubt that timpani sound better at the back of the stage in the centre. Equally, it is helpful to place trombones and trumpets so that they do not project directly into the audience when their sound will blend less well with the rest of the orchestra. The horns project much of their sound backwards. What they are blowing into can critically affect their sound and the orchestral balance. If they have a hard reflective surface behind them, they may easily become overbearing. On the other hand, if they are playing into an absorbent surface (in multi-use theatres, there are often all too many of them!), their sound may become muffled and less effective. Then there is the question of the harp. If the harp is side on to the audience, it makes the player look one-armed but it is not often easy to arrange matters so that the instrument is facing down the hall.

A final controversy relates to the double basses. There is something visually and aurally splendid about a row of basses along the back of the orchestra stage which provides a splendid harmonic framework both for players and audience but it can leave the basses isolated from the 'cello section to whom they have to relate closely. If you are going to propose such a layout, you may need to muster considerable powers of persuasion to get the basses to accept it.

Choral Conducting

I firmly believe that conducting choirs is one of the most enjoyable activities available to a conductor. With an amateur choir, one will often have the opportunity to build a long-term relationship. I had the privilege of forty years with the Guildford Choral Society; my relationship with the City of London Choir is over thirty years old and happily still going strong, and even with the Holst Singers, I enjoyed a fifteen-year association These relationships are not unlike marriages: you learn each other's strengths and weaknesses – the latter can sometimes become a source of mutual irritation, but in a good relationship, both sides develop considerable loyalty and understanding. The Holst Singers commissioned the printing of some pencils (essential for every choral singer) with the words, 'Total Commitment' written on them, as they had heard that phrase so many times at rehearsals! Above all, the permanent conductor has the opportunity to improve standards over the years, while exploring repertoire that can expand both the choir and the conductor's horizons in a genuinely creative way. Of course, there are some professional orchestra/conductor relationships which do very much the same thing: Sir John Barbirolli's work with The Hallé, Sir Simon Rattle's work in Birmingham, and Sir Adrian Boult's extraordinary stint with the BBC Symphony Orchestra (of which he was the first conductor) all testify to the artistic fruits of a long-term association. Nonetheless, the conductor/choir relationship is one of the most rewarding available, if the 'chemistry' works. Amateur singers choose to work with a conductor; professional players very often have a conductor imposed upon them. Inevitably, that changes the dynamic of the relationship.

Amateur choirs

Most choirs in the UK and United States are amateur. At its best, this means skilled musicians who earn a living by another means but love their choral singing with real passion. At its least good, it means singers who are reluctant to work outside their rehearsals – or sometime even within them! A conductor must be more than a competent musician in such a situation; you need qualities of vision, warmth, patience and humanity. There are many excellent musicians who failed to win over a choir because they were unprepared to recognise the need to engage with their singers outside of rehearsals. I have seen a conductor open his laptop at the beginning of a rehearsal break and ignore singers clearly anxious to speak with him; this is unlikely to create the right atmosphere for a good relationship. On the other hand, Richard Farnes, my successor but one with the Milton Keynes Chorale, undertook a parachute jump to raise money for the choir, which made a splendid impression on them, as well as providing funds for a fine performance of Britten's *War Requiem*. This is not to say that every conductor needs to engage in hazardous activities on behalf of their organisation, but that any music director will need to commit beyond the podium to be successful.

Rehearsing choirs

Rehearsing choirs is a different process to rehearsing instrumentalists. The basics of gesture are, of course, the same but a choral conductor needs to have some understanding of the fundamentals of singing, just as the orchestral conductor needs an understanding of the basic principles of string technique. Vocalists generally need to warm up before they embark upon serious rehearsal; a knowledge of some enjoyable, but effective, exercises for doing this is very helpful. Choirs need time to breathe, and continuous reminders of the demands of the text that will connect them to the audience. (There are some fascinating examples of detailed training to be found on YouTube with the renowned choral director, Robert Shaw, creator of the magnificent Robert Shaw Chorale in Atlanta, Georgia.) The conductor also needs to decide whether the singers should stand throughout the rehearsal – tiring, but better for good vocal technique – or alternate with periods of sitting and standing. (The age of your singers may be a factor in this calculation, though no conductor would be foolish enough to mention that.)

There are many practical considerations with amateur choirs that do not exactly correlate with orchestras. Communication is at the heart of all that we do as musicians but 'telling the story' is a particular challenge for those whose musical medium includes words. Solo singers too need to be exceptionally mindful of communicating their text to everyone in the hall. 'All musicians must be actors' is a phrase I have frequently repeated in rehearsals. It is twice as true with singers as with instrumentalists. That said, choral singers' commitment can sometimes translate unhelpfully into rhythmic movements of the head or trunk, which go beyond a desirable sense of enthusiasm. Such mannerisms can become both wearisome and distracting for the audience. Sometimes, a word either with the individual or with the chorus master (if there is one) is necessary to prevent this disturbing the concert. Every choir is a coalition; there will be those for whom improving technical quality is the central goal, others who want a congenial evening to have an agreeable sing with their friends. Obviously, the best choirs have many more of the first category; the less good ensembles, more of the second group. However, every choir will have a mixture of both and the conductor must be not only aware of this, but able to satisfy both groups without alienating any individual member of the choir. You must be critical where necessary but not bullying. Most of all, you must be willing to give the choir a warm smile when something goes unexpectedly well.

Choral conducting needs even more highly developed radar than any other variety. You may be admired and respected by the choir but still unaware of the fact that they are now singing flat because they are simply physically exhausted. Rehearsing intonation in that circumstance merely ensures frustration. On another occasion, however, the same flat singing will simply be a matter of group complacency which might require you to be slightly sharp-edged to elicit the right response. It all depends on the conductor's instant assessment of the group dynamic. We will all get that wrong from time to time but choirs are forgiving if they are sure that the conductor's motivation is their enjoyment and proficiency. It is always important to help them to see that your duty to the composer is what is driving your relentless pursuit of the best possible standard, and not some personal vanity or control freak tendency!

Another obvious difference between the singer and the instrumentalist arises from the fact that the singer's instrument is inside their body. However unwell you feel, you can – with enough determination – make a reasonable sound upon a clarinet, if you are a gifted player. Sadly a singer with a cold is not likely to be able to produce a good tone and the conductor needs to be sympathetic to this. Choirs are also places where it is easier for one singer to infect another because of droplet transmission. It is wise to discourage people from coming if they have respiratory infections – even though their enthusiasm and determination may be, in principle, admirable.

Choice of repertoire

Repertoire choice is another crucial element in the choral conductor's duties (see also 'Programme Planning', page 21). Too much familiar music tends to lead towards complacency; too many challenges can discourage the less confident singer. That dilemma naturally extends to the audience who are much more likely to come to a Bach Passion than to Tippett's *A Child of Our Time* – despite the fact that both speak directly to the hearts of the audience. Indeed, the chorale after Christ's death in the *St Matthew Passion* is closely mirrored by the appearance of 'Deep River' at the end of the Tippett. These are moments where the combination of words and music can – indeed should – be overwhelming for an audience. If you are a musical director of a choir, you will generally need to vary the diet carefully. The season should include at least one well-loved work that the choir can sell to their audience without much difficulty. Equally, at least one work in the season should be new to the choir as far as possible so that each year, long-serving members widen their repertoire and stylistic understanding. You may find that your choir committee wants to be involved in programme planning. Clearly they have a right to ensure that your repertoire choices do not have negative financial consequences. That said, programming by committee seldom works well and the Music Director needs to ensure that the general direction of travel is one chosen by him or herself. Of course, if you consistently choose music the choir does not wish to sing, your days as Music Director will probably be numbered.

There used to be a tradition in some choirs, particularly in the north of England, of singing Handel's *Messiah* annually. I had the pleasure of conducting several of these, both with the Bradford Choral Society and the Leicester Philharmonic Choir. These performances bring their own combination of joys and frustrations. Many of the singers in both choirs could sing the majority of the choruses from memory. As a consequence, their communication with the audience was very powerful. On the other hand, it was a tricky business to embark upon any attempt to change the style, in terms of note lengths or shaping. One had to be careful not to make the mistake of taking the watch to pieces and being unable to put it together in the timeframe available. (See also, 'Guest Conducting', page 63.) Another potential pitfall was the issue of which sections should be cut and which included. This generally is, and definitely should be, entirely a matter for the conductor. Since we now know that Handel himself approved multiple versions of his *Messiah*, we can have a reasonably free hand in selecting the numbers that make the most musical and dramatic coherence. Sometimes one may choose a chorus that has not been sung for many years by the choir; suddenly, the complete confidence with which they are singing most of the work can disappear in a few seconds. If you do select a less familiar number, it is wise to allow some extra rehearsal for it. It is also crucial, of course, to ensure that your soloists are clearly aware of which version of each aria you have chosen. On one occasion, I had listed the aria 'Thou art gone up on high' in the alto version. It emerged in the middle of the rehearsal that the alto had not grasped this; it was deeply fortunate that the bass did know the number and he bravely stepped in, though it involved a bit of speedy editing from the orchestra!

Period performance

This is a good moment to look at the issue of period performance. It is increasingly unwise to perform Baroque music with modern instruments at modern pitch. Audiences are much more aware nowadays of the benefits of period instruments and authentic pitch; it is also very helpful for a choir to collaborate with such orchestras who will transmit useful insights into phrasing and articulation without the conductor needing to speak about it at all. Any choir, however modest in its aspirations, needs to have some grasp of style; to sing Fauré's Requiem and Bach's *St John Passion* with identical articulation and vocal colour, is simply inadequate. Learning to shorten and shape the articulation in the latter while singing a beautiful sustained legato in the former is as valuable for the needs of the choir as it is to the satisfaction of the audience.

Let me add an aside here for all conductors. We can all too easily fall into a fixed view of how the standard choral works should be presented. I always try hard to listen to other conductors' performances of standard repertoire and see what I can learn from them; equally, I try to prepare even a *Messiah* performance with a careful re-examination of my view of the work. If you are performing a work in which you make necessary cuts (which should not happen very often), consider changing the numbers you omit every time you perform the piece de novo.

An obvious benefit of Baroque pitch is that the strain it puts upon the soprano and tenor singers is manifestly less than at modern pitch. Sometimes it is wise to rehearse demanding repertoire down a semitone if your accompanist has the necessary skills, even if your performance is going to be at A=440. (See also 'Rehearsals', page 30.) The adrenaline that will appear in the choir on the day of the concert will carry them up a semitone without difficulty, generally speaking. With the City of London Choir, our preparation of the Bach Passions was for many years, accompanied by Mark Williams (now Informator Choristarum at Magdalen College, Oxford). He actively enjoyed demonstrating his ability at transposition – which was formidable – and it was very helpful for the choir who clearly preferred the darker colour of the slightly less demanding experience provided by the lower pitch.

The issue of pitch is one that could occupy several chapters of choral conducting discussion. It is a fact that G major, A major and B major are harder keys for a choir to remain on pitch than G flat, A flat or B flat. So even with modern a cappella music, I sometimes transpose these a semitone lower. Even a relatively simple Christmas hymn such as 'Once in Royal David's City' is far better in G flat than in G. I have never known a performance in the former key go out of tune, even with quite inexperienced choirs; in G, there is always a slight frisson of apprehension if the first three verses are unaccompanied and the organ or orchestra join you for verse 4! (That is not to say that this is a rule; it is simply my empirical experience.)

Language is another consideration. Just as it was harder to rehearse Stephen Oliver's *Prometheus* with the Guildford Choral Society with its ancient Greek text, so pieces like Bernstein's *Chichester Psalms* need the conductor to be completely on top of the Hebrew for the rehearsals to be productive. I always tried to recruit a language coach for any text written outside the usual English, German, Italian, French or Latin that one can reasonably expect most choral singers to have mastered. Notwithstanding that, when recording Beethoven's much neglected but rather splendid *Der Glorreiche Augenblick* with the City of London Choir and the RPO, a native German speaker saved much time in rehearsals by being able to demonstrate the exact sound required for any difficult phrases. German vowel sounds are very different from English vowels and the best ways to master them is by listening to an authentic model.

Engaging a Vocal Consultant

One of the duties of the choral conductor is to develop the vocal skills of his or her choir. If you are a highly trained singer, you can obviously do it yourself. If not, it is wise to have a vocal consultant if your choir has the resources to engage one. In Guildford, we recruited Margaret Humphrey Clark, who had a profound effect upon the choir's tonal range and quality. She was an exceptional teacher (I subsequently appointed her head of singing at St Paul's Girls' School where she had a similar effect) but she also had a most engaging personality in front of the choir and gave them added confidence. We adopted the same strategy with the City of London Choir, which has Rachel Nicholls as its vocal consultant. Rachel is, of course, an internationally renowned soloist; she is also an exceptional teacher and coach. During the COVID-19 pandemic of 2020, her capacity to teach productively via Zoom played a major part in sustaining the choir's morale.

Accompanists

The person upon whom the conductor will rely most, however, is the choir accompanist. I have generally been very fortunate in mine; on the rare occasions when the accompanist has been inadequate, the effect has been very unhelpful. When I took over both the Guildford and London choirs, neither had a first-class accompanist, but choirs are admirably loyal and it was not easy to persuade them to encourage their accompanists to retire. I was fortunate in both cases to have a chairman who saw the problem and helped to deal with it; the moment we were able to recruit a skilled accompanist, the productivity of rehearsals sharply improved. The best accompanists are worth their weight in gold. They tend to fall into two classes: those who are principally pianists and those who are principally organists. The latter are likely to be more effective at taking sectional rehearsals: the former may well make a more beautiful sound. Very occasionally, you meet someone who combines both qualities. True accompanists will have wonderful ears as well as wonderful fingers. Timothy End, who accompanies the City of London Choir, shapes every phrase impeccably; he is subtly showing the choir how to make music without any words needing to be said. If the conductor and accompanist trust each other enough, a certain amount of mutual teasing can enliven the rehearsal. I have been very lucky to collaborate with musicians like Tim, David Gibson, Mark Williams, Stephen Farr and most recently, Richard Gowers, with whom every rehearsal is enlivened by a bit of badinage. All of them will instantly respond to a slight movement of the tempo, which also encourages the choir to watch more closely. At its best, the interaction between conductor, accompanist and singers can be a masterclass in unspoken communication, similar to that of a finely honed cricket team.

Founding a choir

Finally, what do you do if you are singer or would-be conductor and you find yourself with no choir in your area? The simple answer is to start one! The transformative effects of singing in a choir are well-documented, and starting a choir is definitely easier than starting an orchestra. You need only enthusiasm and one or two friends and supporters. I have had the pleasure of founding two choirs: the Milton Keynes Chorale in 1974 and the Holst Singers in 1978. Happily, both are still thriving without me!

In Milton Keynes, we were fortunate to have the support of the Milton Keynes Development Corporation whose Arts Manager at the time, Cindy Hargate, was happy to use her budget to support musical initiatives. My links to the parents of children who were members of the music centre also helped, of course. Our first performance, of Britten's *St Nicolas*, involved a choir of fifty; five years later there were over a hundred for Vaughan Williams' *A Sea Symphony*. The Chorale's roster of conductors since its foundation is striking: my successor was Simon Halsey, who was followed by Richard Farnes and then Neville Creed. Mark Jordan, the current conductor maintains the standard splendidly, and the Chorale is fast approaching its fiftieth anniversary.

The Holst Singers was and continues to be a different kind of ensemble. A group of friends and contemporaries recently graduated from the universities of Oxford and St Andrews asked me to help them form a chamber choir; we were able to rehearse in the Singing Hall at St Paul's Girls' School, designed by Gustav Holst. It seemed natural to attach his name to the choir, and Imogen Holst graciously agreed to be its first president. The choir thrived and made its first recording for Hyperion Records, including Bliss' *Pastoral* (a much underrated work) and music by Britten and Holst, within five years of its first rehearsal. Under the distinguished leadership of Stephen Layton it is now one of the finest choirs in the country, and has an outstanding discography.

Not every choir can have quite that success, but social media makes it easier to locate like-minded people in a particular location. You just need to find a rehearsal venue and get hold of some music to sing, and off you go. Any competent singer can take a rehearsal at a level that at least enables a group to sing. The possibilities are legion, and you will be surprised by how many ex-singers come out of the shadows if they hear of your group. What you will need is a good treasurer who can keep the accounts in order and ensure that proper budgeting prevents any financial embarrassment. (The Holst Singers had no subscription for the first year of its existence; we soon discovered that that was a mistake.)

Sadly, choral singing is no longer quite as widespread as it was in the 1920s when male-voice choirs in Wales and the north of England provided solace to thousands of unemployed workers during the Great Depression. Nonetheless, the wonderful success of the Military Wives Choirs – un-auditioned, open access and with no age restrictions of any kind – demonstrates unequivocally the power of singing to develop confidence, friendships and wellbeing. In the famous words (manifestly intended to be wholly gender-neutral!) of the great Renaissance composer, William Byrd:

Since singing is so good a thing, I wish all men would learn to sing.[1]

---

[1] *Psalmes, Sonets, & Songs* (1588)

Orchestral Accompaniment

Orchestral accompaniment is a specialised skill and one that is often neglected by conducting teachers. Some of my colleagues seem to believe that a concerto requires less attention than a symphony or a tone poem; nothing could be further from the truth. The final rehearsal must offer the soloist the chance to play every note of the concerto if he or she so wishes – and most do. A normal orchestral concert benefits hugely from the presence of a soloist who will add to the drama of the performance in a profound way. The conductor also has the pleasure – and generally, it is a pleasure – of another musical mind deeply invested in the particular work at hand.

Preparation

Whenever possible, I try to ensure a meeting with the soloist before the day of the concert. Hearing the concerto played through (with piano, if appropriate) is enormously helpful. There is little more vexatious than playing a long orchestral introduction and then hearing the soloist enter with a completely different set of phrasings or bowings from those the orchestra has just played. If there is a disagreement on such matters – or even on tempo – it is my unequivocal view that the soloist's wish must prevail. The conductor should try to merge into the shadows in a concerto performance and should act as a 'sponge' during the rehearsal, to soak up the soloist's concept of the piece. I have heard many unedifying performances where there has been a tangible disagreement between soloist and conductor – at every entry of the tutti, the pulse moves slightly forwards or backwards and the integrity of the piece is undermined. There are places – the long scale in the last movement of Beethoven's Piano Concerto No. 4, Op. 58, for example – that are genuinely difficult for the conductor to place exactly. The safest solution for the conductor is to anticipate a little. To obliterate the last two or three notes of a run can scarcely be argued to be the most musical outcome, but the alternative – of a tiny gap before the orchestral entry – is worse. The best solution is that the soloist and conductor should both seek to take care of each other in such tricky moments. To be exactly on time at a difficult corner is one of the occasions when a conductor may justifiably feel a moment of self-satisfaction.

I once saw Vernon Handley moving his tongue exactly in time with the nineteen rapid notes proceeding an orchestral entry in a Chopin piano concerto. Unsurprisingly, he brought the orchestra in at exactly the right moment but not every conductor will have that speed of response. Here, as in so many places, a deep knowledge of the soloist's part is very important; we must not neglect to learn that as thoroughly as the orchestral material. It is equally helpful that the soloist shall know the orchestral part intimately. Working with soloists of the calibre of Peter Donohoe or Stephen Hough, one can always been certain that they would be able to play the orchestral part with the same detailed memory as their own. There are other soloists with whom that will be less certain. One soloist in a Mozart piano concerto had written her own cadenza which actually resolved onto the wrong chord at the end; of course, this came to light in the rehearsal, but it made for an uneasy moment in the concert as she tried to negotiate the last-minute change we had patched up together.

Most soloists prefer to be called late in the final rehearsal, but the conductor must check this as some require a period of rest before the concert. Brass and wind soloists, in particular, will probably want time for their lips to recover; singers vary but will expect – rightly – to have their wishes observed.

Challenges

Many soloists have strong musical personalities; some of them can be quite difficult. If there are linguistic difficulties, this can add stress to rehearsals. This is one of the important reasons why a rehearsal prior to the concert day can be very useful. If a conductor meets an international soloist for the first time at 4.00 p.m. on the day of the concert, it inevitably puts some pressure on the rehearsal. On one occasion, my first collaboration with the wonderful Bulgarian violinist, Stoika Milanova, her agent had foolishly arranged for her to travel by train from Newcastle to Milton Keynes for a Beethoven concert that evening. She arrived at the hall looking visibly edgy and smoking two cigarettes simultaneously; something I have never seen before or since. Her English was not very good, my Bulgarian non-existent, so we had to communicate in French, which was the second language for us both. After a sticky start, we established a rapport. She was palpably tense as we began to rehearse but it was inspiriting to watch her relax as the long orchestral introduction to the concerto unfolded before her first entry. It was very fortunate that the Milton Keynes City Orchestra players were determined to be helpful and gave extra attention to the quality of their playing (which I would not normally have asked for in a rehearsal) to convince this great artist that she was going to have an enjoyable evening with serious collaborators. She paid us the ultimate tribute of staying for the second half of the concert to hear Beethoven's Symphony No. 5, Op. 67, which concluded the evening. I was therefore able to drive her back to her Bulgarian 'safehouse' in London afterwards. The journey was fascinating and I learned much about life for a musician behind the Iron Curtain. Such moments compensate for all the disappointments musicians inevitably experience from time to time.

There can be other unexpected issues for the conductor to manage. A congenial soloist may still reveal unexpected qualities – both negative and positive – in performance. Some will change tempi substantially between rehearsal and concert, others ignore carefully rehearsed rubato and plough straight on; yet others allow nerves to inflect the performance in a number of unpredictable ways. Performing Beethoven's Piano Concerto No. 4, Op. 58, with the distinguished pianist, Peter Katin, in a concert in Milton Keynes in the 1980s, provided a dramatic example of this. We had a slightly tricky rehearsal, as he was visibly rather jittery and did not much care for the Steinway piano the promoter had hired for him to play. We managed to make the piece work, however, and I was fairly confident we would have a good show. He made an exceptionally beautiful sound, despite his reservations about the piano. Hence I was taken aback when, as we stood in the wings at the concert before going on to the platform, he said, 'I can't go on, I can't go on'. I had about five seconds to consider the options; I certainly could not play the piece myself, nor was I going to tell the audience that the soloist was not appearing. My only alternative was to push him forcibly onto the platform! This was what I did. Peter reached the piano slightly unsteadily, bowed, and proceeded to play an immaculate performance. When I rang his agent the next day to tell him that I had almost had a nervous breakdown, he said, 'Yes, Peter sometimes does that!', whereupon I remarked tartly that it would have been helpful to have had some warning of this possibility. Clearly some performers, including a number of the very best, pay a high psychological price every time they face an audience. Adrian Boult told me that Yehudi Menuhin, with whom he collaborated on numerous occasions, became very nervous before a concert and often played better at the final rehearsal that in the show itself.

Other soloists, on the other hand, seem to have nerves of steel. Piers Lane gave the premier of a complex new work by Dave Heath that included a cadenza with cascades of notes for the piano, requiring exact coordination with two percussion players. Before we went on, Piers chatted amiably to me about the contrast between England and Australia. He then marched cheerfully onto the platform and proceeded to dispatch this daunting piece with relish.

A further potential challenge for the conductor may be having to deal with changes in personnel at short notice. This is bad enough in the orchestra. To have one's first oboe or first trumpet player become ill on the day before the concert provokes anxiety; you must decide whether to ask the second player to play principal or to invite a guest first player at short notice, who may or may not fit in with the rest of the section. The decision you make will materially affect the experience of both your audience and your orchestra, but you have to make it quickly.

The indisposition of a soloist is yet more serious. Live music is like walking on a tightrope without a safety net. Some attacks of illness can come perilously close to the concert. I once had a performance in Guildford of Elgar's wonderful but underperformed oratorio *The Kingdom,* for which we had booked Lynne Dawson to sing the crucial soprano part.(It is the soprano who has the greatest aria in the piece, 'The Sun Goeth Down', widely regarded as the finest orchestral aria in the English language.) So it was with consternation that I took a call from Lynne at 11.30 on the morning of the concert in which she told me she was in A&E in a Yorkshire hospital. I could think of only one other soprano, Julie Kennard, who would have the vocal quality to suit the role. I rang her to find her in her kitchen in West London. I asked her if she knew *The Kingdom*. She replied that she had sung it some ten years earlier. She gamely agreed to take on the engagement if I would allow her to be a little late for the rehearsal so that she could at least look through the part before setting off for the cathedral. In the event, she gave one of the finest performances I have ever heard of the work, but if she had been out for the day, I have no idea what I would have done.

The most difficult issues, of course, arise when there is a genuine lack of connection between soloist and conductor. It is the conductor's job to smooth over any problems that arise as a consequence, but this is not always an easy thing to achieve. If the soloist insists on taking over the rehearsal, the conductor does have to make clear that this is a collaboration not an autocracy. On the other hand, if the soloist makes insightful suggestions about the music, the conductor should be grateful and determine to incorporate these into the performance.

There are, inevitably, a number of fine soloists who would like to have conducting careers and often believe (not always rightly) that it is better that they, rather than the conductor, should be in charge. Happily, I have only experienced this on very few occasions. A more dangerous situation arises if the soloist and the orchestra leader have a mutual antipathy. An experienced leader will manoeuvre round this but I remember a difficult moment when the leader and a violin soloist had a sharp exchange over which part of the bow the first violins should use in a particularly quiet passage of accompaniment. This was difficult. As conductor, I naturally wished to support my leader. On the other hand, the soloist was a distinguished musician; with such people, temperament can lead to unpredictable consequences. I had no wish to see him leave the rehearsal in a rage and decline to return! I smoothed it over somehow but I did not make the mistake of inviting the soloist to return.

The question of balance

At the heart of the accompanying process is the question of balance. Some composers make this easier for the conductor than others. Elgar, for example, uses the orchestra with consummate skill in his Cello Concerto, Op. 85, so that there are few moments when the conductor is likely to be required to quieten the orchestra. In Rachmaninov piano concertos, on the other hand, there will be places where you need to interpret the printed dynamic with caution. In particular, brass fortes may need to be scaled down. In many concertos of the romantic period, quite often an orchestral forte may need to be refined to mezzo forte to allow the soloist to come through the texture. This is particularly true when the soloist enters over an orchestral forte, after a period of silence; if the audience miss the detail of such an entry, it can be quite a serious loss.

String soloists have the disadvantage that their tone is less instantly distinguishable from the orchestral strings, who are in close proximity. Some composers are fully aware of this and use the soloist in a totally different register from the tutti, to deal with the problem. Other composers are less insightful. Schumann's Cello Concerto, Op. 129, for example, requires the conductor to be really attentive to matters of balance; there are several places where the orchestra can inadvertently cover the 'cello in its middle register, so the conductor is wise to listen from further back in the hall to check that all is well. It has always baffled me that Schumann's piano concerto is so beautifully scored, yet most of the time the composer seems to be slightly primitive in his use of the orchestra. Of course, he had well-documented problems with conducting, so some of the infelicities will have been to do with safety and numbers, but there is still an enigma here, as the piano concerto shows that he clearly had mastered orchestration.

Singers may also require to be looked after with extra care; even Richard Strauss's *Four Last Songs* – great orchestrator though he was – have moments where the soloist will be swamped if the orchestra plays the printed dynamic. There can be problems even in Baroque music: Handel doubles the bass solos in *Acis and Galatea* with the orchestral bassline much of the time. Even a rumbustious Polyphemus will sometimes struggle if the fortes in the orchestra are taken literally.

The most interesting of all my experience of orchestral/solo balance came in Milton Keynes when we had the pleasure of accompanying Richard Burnett on a fortepiano, from the famous Finchcocks' collection, in Mozart's Piano Concerto No. 12, K. 414. Richard was a sensitive artist but the dynamic range of the fortepiano is basically pianissimo to mezzo piano. The orchestra, though relatively small, had to scale its dynamics to a completely different soundworld from the usual. It took us about half an hour to internalise the concept that forte meant mezzo piano and piano meant pianissimo, but I am glad to say by the concert this had been achieved. The audience had to listen intently, of course, but in many ways, this was a bonus and we certainly had greater stillness in the hall than we normally achieved. Balance is seldom a question of numbers alone, though having three or four double basses at the bottom of a Mozart concerto is probably asking for trouble. The key issue is simply the need for everybody to listen. If the orchestra cannot hear the soloist clearly, it is highly likely that the audience will not be able to either.

One further principle needs to be mentioned. It is always a mistake to have the piano between the orchestra and its conductor. A false aural picture is created in that position as the piano will mask much of the orchestral sound. If you stand between the orchestra and the pianist, you have a much better sense of the true balance.

Some conductors, Sir Thomas Beecham among them, did not much enjoy accompanying and were happier when they were in complete control of proceedings. For me, a collaboration with a musical partner with whom I feel a genuine connection is often the high point of a performance. Student conductors would be well advised to seek out opportunities to conduct soloists so that this skill can be developed alongside all other conductorial techniques.

Final thoughts

Looking back over my career, the most exciting moments of over fifty years' work have been those when a soloist – sometimes vocal, sometimes instrumental – has somehow conveyed an unequivocal sense of what they wanted from the conductor at a subliminal, but yet unmistakable, level. Such moments are, by definition, rare; they produce an exceptional sense of intimacy. It would be invidious to mention individuals but inevitably, there are colleagues with whom one has an especially close rapport from the first moment. I have always tried to ensure that we have more than one chance to collaborate in such a circumstance. Some of my musical partnerships have lasted almost fifty years and are among my most treasured friendships.

The best of all worlds, of course, is to be on a tour with someone whose music-making gives you delight: feeling a performance grow and deepen during a series of four or five concerts is a source of satisfaction rarely vouchsafed to the musician – though more accessible, I suppose, for actors involved in a long run of daily performances. The Milton Keynes Orchestra made a tour of the United States in the 1990s with the American pianist, Steven Lubin, playing Beethoven's Piano Concerto No. 2, Op. 19. Each performance added an extra layer of subtlety and nuance to the collaboration; I was genuinely sad to leave the platform with him for the last time, knowing that we were unlikely to work again for several years. Learning of my distaste for long distance coach travel, Steven had volunteered to drive me from Philadelphia to New York and we had wonderful conversations about music and indeed, life. I am absolutely clear that this resulted in a more rewarding experience, both for us and the audience, at our final performance together.

Touring

Touring with a choir or orchestra is a very different experience from playing in or near your home base. On the one hand, you are likely to have a more limited repertoire and several chances to play or sing most of it. On the other hand, your musicians may get fatigued or if you are touring with young people, even start to feel homesick. On a tour, self-control, both regarding sex and alcohol, can be lost and the consequences are generally unhelpful. There is seldom very much time for sightseeing or other enjoyable tourist activities as a lot of time will be spent on a bus or a train. All that said, I know nothing likely to improve artistic quality more swiftly than that intensive experience of making music together that a tour provides.

It is sensible to try to do most of the rehearsing before you commence the tour. Rehearsing on a tour is always likely to be more complicated than anticipated. Trains or boats can be late, arrangements at halls not always well-organised and there are often tricky acoustics to be negotiated. Simply having time for the musicians to become familiar with the stage, the sight lines and what they can actually hear on the platform, is often the most you can achieve.

Touring abroad

When the Milton Keynes City Orchestra made its very successful tour of the Eastern Seaboard of the United States in 1994, we arrived at New York's Carnegie Hall to set up for a Saturday afternoon concert to be told that the technicians and stage hands had just begun a sixty-minute lunchbreak and would, in no circumstances, begin to set up for us until every minute of it was past. This was not unreasonable, except that nobody had mentioned it when suggesting our arrival time! Unfortunately, we had arrived quite early and had decided to go to lunch before we settled into the hall; that turned out to be an unwise decision. In these circumstances, all you can do is get on with it as best you can. Our manager tried to see if there was any way of accelerating the process but it was clear that the workforce had a resolutely inflexible approach. In this situation, the conductor must radiate calm and good will, and I worked hard to achieve this, with only moderate success. In the event, our rehearsal was reduced by a third, but as so often with British players, the musicians worked at great pace to get to grips with the acoustic and 'play into' the hall. It was a decent concert with a surprisingly large audience; American audiences discern very little difference between Milton Keynes and Manchester so that the slightly modest resonances of our name meant little to most of them. For all our success though, the pressure put on our already brief rehearsal meant that it was all rather stressful and unsurprisingly, many players went off for an extended drink at four o'clock in the afternoon when the concert had finished! A more disquieting development was the disappearance for twenty-four hours of our principal bassoon player, John Whitfield, a magnificent musician of somewhat wayward personal habits. I was seriously worried he might be difficult to track down, but somehow he arrived – looking pretty dishevelled, but otherwise fine, to join the bus the next day. The conductor cannot stand entirely aloof from welfare issues; it is you who will have to contend with a gap in an orchestra if someone goes missing, or try to galvanise players with a bad hangover or an emotional overload. It would be easy to see this all as a management problem, but if you are not concerned for your players' welfare, that can easily become mutual.

With choirs, the problems are slightly different. Each singer carries their instrument with them; if people drink too much, go to bed too late (or not at all), the effect on the voice will be discernible sooner rather than later. On the other hand, amateur singers are giving up their valuable holidays to come to sing and they do not wish to be wholly occupied by the music. This is a delicate balancing act that the conductor must navigate carefully.

The Holst Singers had some splendid tours; in 1982 (fewer than four years after the choir had been formed), we were invited to the famous Summer Music Festival in Siena, to celebrate its fiftieth anniversary. We planned other concerts in Tuscany around this engagement, including a performance in the Duomo in Florence. All went reasonably well until we arrived in Siena. The train from Florence was late so we arrived slightly breathless at the Palazzo Chigi-Saracini. This houses the magnificent Rococo-style concert hall, splendidly restored by the architect, Arturo Viligiardi, which contains an equally magnificent organ – at least, so it appeared. We had been asked to perform three of Handel's coronation anthems and two major Britten pieces – the unaccompanied *Hymn to St Cecilia* and *Rejoice in the Lamb,* with its demanding organ part. We brought with us as organist Philip Moore, at that time organist at York Minster and one of the finest accompanists of his generation. On arrival, we enquired of the porter how the organ was to be turned on; he shrugged and said, 'Organ no go – organ no go for five years'. This was something of a setback. The coronation anthems all had accompaniments as crucial as in the Britten. It would have been fruitless to rehearse without them. The porter, though perfectly affable, clearly had no response to my question as to what we should do next; but he did vouchsafe the information that the Director would be back after lunch. It was by now approaching noon, at which point, the building would apparently be closed. The Singers were perfectly relaxed about the situation, of course. They could see a long lunch with relatively cheap wine in prospect, whereas I could only see problems! I enquired when the building would reopen and was told 4.00 p.m. – a very Mediterranean interpretation of the lunch 'hour'.

Shortly after 4.00 p.m. the singers began to arrive back in the hall and the Director finally made his appearance. Philip and I pointed out the difficulty of the concert without an organ. The Director smiled benignly and replied, 'No problem, we have organo electronico, I will go and fetch it'. He returned carrying a five-octave Yamaha keyboard! There was a moment of impasse, but we were being paid a very substantial fee for the concert, without which the tour would not have been viable, so something had to be cobbled together. Eventually, we used a harpsichord for the Handel – stylistically appropriate, but wholly inaudible whenever the choir sang – and a piano for the Britten, with the organ pedal part being played at the bottom of the piano by a member of the choir. It was manifestly unsatisfactory but the audience seemed entirely unworried and gave us a standing ovation. There is something to be said for the relaxed Mediterranean temperament!

Our other tours managed to avoid anything quite so dramatic, though there was an occasion in Norway when, as we approached a fjord, we saw our ferry leaving the jetty. This threatened to truncate our rehearsal time, but the driver responded by using his radio to contact the captain who promptly turned the ship back and waited for us to board ten minutes later. I have been a fan of Norwegian ferries ever since! (Norwegian promoters were markedly more efficient than their Italian counterparts, but the Singers did not like the high cost of wine and beer.)

Keeping musicians focused during tours can be challenging, but there is no doubt that giving a series of concerts in a short space of time raises standards and is often uniquely rewarding. Emotional dramas are seldom far away, however, and sometimes need careful handling. I have known couples, married and otherwise, whose relationships begin to fracture under the pressures of a tour. It is difficult – and probably unwise – of a conductor to intervene in any way at all. On the other hand, tension generated inside the touring group can put performance standards at risk so one should certainly do one's best to keep things calm. Equally problematic can be the emergence of 'tour romances' between two choir members who have other partners, or even spouses, back home. I tried resolutely to cultivate an air of blissful ignorance about all these excitements but it was always a potential source of anxiety. My advice to young conductors is to try to avoid entanglements with musicians they are going to direct. The reputational damage may or may not be significant but any suggestion that one musician may occupy a special place in the conductor's affections is liable to provoke jealousies and often disapproval. All of which is intensified in the slightly hothouse atmosphere of a tour. Inevitably, emotional confusion on the part of the conductor will militate against artistic success and provide an unhelpful distraction from the task in hand.

Adjusting to strange acoustics can sometimes be exceptionally challenging for visiting performers. When the Guildford Choral Society made its first trip to Brussels in 1994, we had scheduled a performance of Duruflé's Requiem in the Basilique Nationale du Sacré-Coeur. This is a most impressive building, but the performance area provided for us at the end of the nave was a very long way from the organ console, which was elevated and without any direct sightline to the conductor. In most English cathedrals, one would expect to have some kind of microphone and television link to the organist in such a situation. In the Sacré-Coeur, none such were provided. Even with electronic aids, it is still a tricky business to accompany at a distance but an experienced organist will generally cope with it. Here, an extraordinary feat of anticipation and lightning response to the sound was required. We were exceptionally fortunate to have brought Richard Pearce with us to play the organ part – a demanding role at the best of times. The rehearsal had started late because our coach had been delayed by heavy traffic caused by an international football match, coinciding with our rehearsal. It was all really quite fraught, with a particular difficulty in the 'Pie Jesu' movement in which the fine 'cellist, Alison Moncrieff-Kelly, had come to join us. She, of course, had to be close to our mezzo-soprano soloist, Jacqueline Varsey, at the front of the stage; it was even harder for the organist to accompany just two musicians at a distance of almost 40 metres! Richard's exceptional accompanying skills, however, rose to the occasion; I was genuinely able to forget about the distance because he anticipated with such skill. Of course, any conductor in that situation is wise to reduce his rhythmical *rubati* to a minimum. Any interpretative quirk that makes ensemble playing more difficult may need to be constrained in such a circumstance. The key point is that whatever the difficulties: visibility, audibility, heating, uncomfortable or even absent seating for the choir, it is the conductor's job to convince everyone that the performance will be fine. It does underline the need for thorough musical preparation before any tour begins. If there are unsolved technical problems in the performance, you are unlikely to find time or opportunity to solve many of them in a strange building while touring. (There was a happy sequel to our trip to Brussels. It ushered in a delightful and continuing collaboration with the Brussels Choral Society, a fine and very international choir. Joint performances of Verdi's Requiem in both in Brussels and Guildford, and Walton's *Belshazzar's Feast* in London's Royal Albert Hall, were happy sequels to our Belgian expedition.)

Touring closer to home

It is not essential, of course, to tour to a foreign country – though I suspect musicians find it more interesting to do so. I developed with the Guildford Choral Society (GCS) a biennial 'Residential Weekend' pattern which proved a great success with the singers. We always brought along our vocal consultant, Margaret Humphrey Clark, and worked on some specific repertoire as well as general choral techniques. The Saturday evening was traditionally left free for social activities which were very good for increasing the *esprit de corps* of the choir. It also gave me a chance to get to know choir members better which was helpful. I think that everybody felt that these weekends raised standards in a measurable way.

At the end of my last GCS choral weekend, we went to the beautiful Priory at Boxgrove in West Sussex and gave an informal concert. We had been 'in residence' at a college in Chichester; to our surprise and delight, our normal modest audience of families and friends who came to the weekend's traditional final performance was much increased by staff and other residents from the college, who had heard the choir rehearsing. The beauty of the surroundings at Boxgrove certainly provoked the choir to a more intense performance than we usually achieved at the end of a weekend. This serves to illustrate that here are so many factors that can influence the quality of a performance and not all of them are purely musical.

When I became conductor of the City of London Choir (CLC), we developed the same pattern. The CLC's vocal consultant, Rachel Nicholls, was again a major participant and, indeed, managed to give some individual lessons as well as her invaluable work in warming up the choir and ensuring that singers used their voices well. As the CLC has many young members, social activities were sometimes rather more raucous than with the GCS. A 'human pyramid' became a CLC tradition on the Saturday night; clearly not a risk-assessed activity! Despite this strenuous social life, the singers achieved a great deal through their intensive rehearsals and I believe every choir should consider providing something of the sort on a regular basis. There is nothing that can simultaneously raise both standards and morale in quite the same way.

Youth orchestra tours

Touring is obviously a good experience for young players in a raft of ways. They will have time to experience their host countries, at the least to some extent, and very few will fail to have their horizons significantly broadened by the experience. Youth orchestra tours are easier than professional tours in some ways, but harder in others. On the one hand, the conductor will not be responsible for the young musicians' welfare, except in the most generalised way. There will be pastoral staff and instrumental coaches attached to the tour who will look after the young musicians and deal with most issues that arise. On the other hand, younger musicians are more likely to develop repetitive stress injuries than their professional counterparts. They are playing far more intensely on a tour than they usually do; it is certainly part of the conductor's role to monitor this and ensure that not too much is asked of the players in terms of rehearsal time. Some of the younger musicians may be away from home for the first time and need very gentle handling in rehearsals. Good radar is essential for any conductor, but particularly important on a tour with young musicians.

The conductor may also be reasonably expected to act in an ambassadorial role. I have been to many pre- and post-concert receptions in British embassies; all have been delightful experiences though some of our hosts have been manifestly less interested in the concert than others. It is always a bonus if the ambassador or their deputy has a clear awareness of the public relations benefit that a good concert can provide. British youth orchestras in the 1980s were probably the best in the world; many of them have since been weakened by 30 years of cuts to the music education budgets in Britain. This is very damaging, not just for the individual student whose potential is not fully realised, but equally unhelpful for the reputation of Britain as a place where young musicians thrive.

Youth Orchestras

General principles

Some of the most satisfying experiences for a conductor are to be found working with young musicians, for whom the excitement of performing repertoire for the first time can be quite special. I always tried to treat a youth orchestra very much as I would a more mature ensemble. It is easy to 'talk down' to young musicians and always a mistake to do so. Student musicians are very quick to detect a patronising tone and they do not like it. There will be occasions when you may need slightly more preparatory beats to achieve an unequivocal ensemble in a tricky opening, and certainly one may need to beat a little more expansively to inspire a full tone when the composer has asked for it. These modifications, however, need to be relatively few and on a small scale; the technical principles of conducting remain unchanged whatever the age of the ensemble you are directing.

There is no more advantage in giving lectures to young orchestras during a rehearsal than in making the same error with a professional ensemble. Only if specifically designed to fire their imaginations about the piece they are rehearsing should verbal communication occupy more than a very small percentage of rehearsal time. It is clearly vital that the conductor has an accurate view of how demanding to be, while remaining relentlessly positive with the players. There will, almost certainly, be occasional moments when being critical is not only necessary, but essential. Young people know if they are not doing their best; if they are told they are 'marvellous' at such times, they will feel patronised and unmotivated. On the other hand, building confidence is the central role for anyone in a management position. If your young players leave the rehearsal feeling daunted, you have failed. More to the point, if they lose motivation, they may well decide to devote themselves to another of the myriad opportunities available to youthful enthusiasts in the twenty-first century. In some orchestras, you may have a viola player who has had only a year or two of lessons. It is part of your job as a conductor to convince such a player that they will be able to make a worthwhile contribution and that they will enjoy doing it. The more limited the technical capacity of your players, the more significant your role in repertoire choice and inspirational leadership. Many very fine conductors do not deal well with young players with limited techniques; in my experience, however, the very best manage it spectacularly well.

At one stage in my career, the principal 'cello of the Leicestershire Schools' Symphony Orchestra (LSSO) became a colleague of mine. He told me an anecdote about when Sir Adrian Boult came to conduct the LSSO. They were to play Beethoven's *Eroica* symphony; Sir Adrian beat the first two bars and stopped. 'Is that the best you can do in Leicester?' he said challengingly, and then started again. The sound that then emerged on the first chord nearly broke the windows in the rehearsal room. That capacity to arouse the enthusiasm of a young ensemble has been mirrored by many fine conductors; Abbado, Barenboim, Giulini and Rattle among them. Sitting in rehearsals with such musicians in charge is a masterclass, not just in conducting, but in inspiring young players. Everyone interested in conducting would benefit from watching these relationships in practice. Sadly, modern considerations of safeguarding make it more difficult for a student to attend rehearsals with youth orchestras nowadays, but parents should certainly go whenever possible, to discover what their children are experiencing. (It will help to lift those moments on a wet November evening when a young 'cellist has to be driven to a school hall five or ten miles from home!)

All of one's work with young players has an immediate goal: to increase the skill and enjoyment gained in rehearsal and performance. There is a final benefit beyond this. Some of the players you are directing will continue into the profession. There is nothing more reassuring when you stand in front of a professional orchestra for the first time than to see one or two smiling faces of players you conducted – or even accompanied – in their student days. Those long days of youth orchestra courses can return something genuinely heartwarming as you observe the skills of your erstwhile young musicians flourishing in a professional context. Obviously, that will not be the goal of the majority of youth orchestra members but even if you have simply broadened some young players' horizons, it will be as good a use of your time as working with a major national ensemble.

Repertoire choice

The youth orchestra conductor must be careful to choose repertoire that is challenging without being over-extending. I have seen too many conductors choose material that they wished to conduct, regardless of the needs of their young players. I have heard over-stretched performances of *Der Rosenkavalier* dances and Brahms' symphonies; pieces that simply asked too much of the orchestra – and clearly were more about conductorial vanity than the musical development of the young players. One of my conducting students was invited to a masterclass with a youth orchestra, in which the repertoire was Strauss' *Don Juan*. Neither she nor the orchestra were capable of doing justice to the piece and it seemed to me an ill-considered repertoire choice. That said, there are many occasions where young musicians can exceed expectation. Twentieth-century music with its often complex rhythms seems to come more easily to young players than their parents, and the quality of woodwind and brass principals may surprise even the experienced conductor.

I have had the pleasure of conducting the National Children's Orchestra (NCO) of Great Britain several times. Some of my repertoire choices worked better than others but I remember a fine performance of Vaughan Williams' ballet, *Job*, in Birmingham Town Hall where the orchestra were genuinely inspired by the music and the glorious climax for organ and timpani was dispatched with conspicuous *élan*. The fact that the timpanist was Ben Glassberg, now a highly successful conductor himself, doubtless helped, but the whole orchestra rose to the challenge of this elusive piece.

For my final concert with the NCO, I was persuaded, slightly against my better judgement, to conduct Elgar's Symphony No. 1. I was torn in two directions: on the one hand, I had studied the piece with Sir Adrian Boult and longed to conduct it; on the other, it is a genuinely taxing piece, even for a professional orchestra. In the event, it was a notable success. The players found the piece bewitching and, as a consequence, they carried it off splendidly. (I have often thought that I would like their performance of the slow movement to be played at my funeral!) The presence of Peter Maxwell Davies' *An Orkney Wedding, With Sunrise* in the first half worked surprisingly well as an aperitif for the richness of the Elgar. Nonetheless, one should err on the side of caution rather than give young musicians a sense that they have not quite delivered with their performance. They are certain to know if they have not achieved a quality show; that is a damaging feeling to take off the concert platform, particularly for youthful players. It is the conductor's job to avoid that outcome at all costs by shrewd repertoire selection.

Orchestral balance

Quite often in youth orchestras you may have doubled or even tripled woodwind. The conductor must take a view about how many of the key orchestral solos will be played by one player and how many tutti passages will have the part played by two or three musicians. There are obvious solos – the cor anglais in the slow movement of Dvořák's Symphony No. 9, for example – where doubling would create a caricature of the composer's intentions but in the sweeping lines of a Brahms tutti, doubling was standard practice in many continental orchestras in the twentieth century and there is absolutely no reason why young players should not play as many notes as possible. It is very boring to sit watching your colleague play an exciting passage when you know you can do it as well as they can, and inside an orchestral forte, it is often an advantage to have doubled wind parts to improve the orchestral balance.

Allocating individual solo passages to several different players can require both tact and political skill. It is generally sensible to leave this to your section coach (they can take any parental flak that may result), but if you feel that one player is being offered too little or another too much, it is important to ensure both fairness and opportunity. Human nature sometimes means that a particular coach finds it difficult to assess objectively the quality of an individual player whose manner may leave something to be desired. The conductor can keep aloof from this but there will be times when intervention is required – as it can be, of course, in a professional orchestra, if personal difficulties are impacting on artistic outcomes. Parental pressure can be another irritant and needs to be resolutely ignored.

A conductor would be wise when conducting young musicians to have made careful disposition in each score as to how many players play at every point. Such decisions may need to be reviewed in light of advice from the wind coaches; asking for such advice is common sense, but decisions about how to create the best sound must ultimately rest with the conductor. Some coaches can become defensive if the conductor seeks to rehearse three or four woodwind or brass players by themselves in a general rehearsal. It is good not to do this very often, but it is important that your musical vision is the one that prevails, and it can be very helpful to use two or three minutes in a rehearsal to get something exactly right. To spend more than a few minutes on one passage is – obviously – to invite the rest of the orchestra to lose interest!

Sectional rehearsals

One difference between preparing a youth orchestra and a professional orchestra for a performance may be the amount of sectional rehearsal that will be advisable. Good instrumental coaches are worth their weight in gold. I have seen many good coaches create a powerful bond of trust that enables their section to improve by leaps and bounds over a week. For a string section, in particular, there may be places where two or three players will simply find the technical demands daunting. A good coach will make whatever small alterations to the notation are necessary in order to make the passage negotiable. The conductor will not have time for this and may not have the knowledge to give the best advice, either. It is sometimes useful in places where there are rapid articulations or tremolando for the inside players to play half the number of the written notes, i.e. quavers instead of semiquavers, or semiquavers in place of demisemiquavers. This has the effect of adding both weight and clarity to the sound of the section. Like all such devices, overuse is a mistake, but it can enormously improve the sound of a young string section in key moments because it gives the players a sense of being in command of the music.

Some youth orchestras have a different rehearsal pattern; a regular weekly rehearsal – generally at a weekend – and these may provide the conductor with less support from instrumental coaches. Some, indeed, may provide none at all. The Ealing Youth Orchestra, which I conducted for three years from 1979, was run by the Local Education Authority (LEA) on a Friday evening. The LEA paid for the hire of a pleasant school hall and a modest fee for the conductor, and left the young players to run everything else for themselves. My predecessor, John Railton, was a fine musician, who actually conducted *The Rite Of Spring* with the orchestra, despite having only one arm, requiring him to stop conducting whenever there was a page to be turned. The young players liked and respected him and they gave an impressive performance of the piece, helped by the fact that a dozen of them were students at the Royal College of Music or Royal Academy of Music. Thankfully, the orchestra's general manager was able to compensate for the administrative deficiencies of her new conductor. I devised a strategy of bringing in a professional soloist to play a concerto at least twice a year and ruthlessly exploited these fine musicians to provide at least some of the coaching that the LEA would not pay for. I particularly remember the principal 'cello of the London Symphony Orchestra, Douglas Cummings, joining us for Dvořák's Cello Concerto, Op. 104. I assured him it would be helpful if he were to rehearse with us on three occasions before the day of the concert. Shamelessly, I scheduled the first one as a strings-only rehearsal and crowbarred him into spending the first half of the evening on the other works in the programme with extensive technical advice – and demonstration – from him. He raised a metaphorical eyebrow but his sunny nature meant that everyone had a productive time and I was able to sit back and listen to the first hour of the rehearsal. Happily, he told me afterwards that he had thoroughly enjoyed the experience.

Rehearsal planning

On a residential orchestra course, you will need a clear plan to give the players a sense of accumulating confidence and mastery. In earlier rehearsals, it is perfectly reasonable to repeat small passages, including at a slower tempo, to help to develop technical competence. As the week goes on, these passages need to be longer; by the last day or two, the players must be allowed to play for at least four or five minutes at a time so that they can begin to grasp the architecture of the work. It is a mistake to arrive at the concert day without having played every piece through uninterrupted at least once in a previous rehearsal. One of the most difficult things for young players is to understand the need to budget their physical strength on the day of a concert. All too often, brass players run out of lip; string players develop soreness in the bowing arm or in the neck muscles where upper string players hold the instrument. This is the conductor's business. You should plan the rehearsal mindful of the inexperience of the players in looking after themselves and ensure that they know how much stamina they require to give their best at the concert. In my experience of residential courses, there were often players who got into physical difficulty because they were unused to playing for more than hour a day during their normal school routine. Suddenly playing for five – or more – hours a day put their bodies under too much strain. It may be sensible to take a short break every forty minutes or so in the rehearsal. You can use the time either to tell an anecdote or to invite the players just to stretch and relax their muscles.

Concert venues

It is crucial to remember that while training is an important part of your work with young people, they also need to have experience of giving concerts in a range of venues. The best of all experiences is an overseas tour where you are able repeat some or all of the repertoire two or three times in different halls. With the Edinburgh Youth Orchestra, I had the pleasure of a tour of Scandinavia that included the extraordinary acoustic of Dalhalla, a magnificent concert arena created out of a disused quarry in Sweden. This was near the end of a five-concert tour; the orchestra were tired, but so riveted by the environment that they played splendidly, aided by natural amplification from the lake and the stone cliffs beyond the platform. (I have wonderful memories of the occasion, only marginally diminished by the fact that my contract specified that I should be rowed to the podium. Since I cannot swim, I found this a daunting prospect! My agitation was not lessened by the two large Swedish ladies in traditional dress who turned out to be my rowers; I cowered in the bottom of the boat praying that I would not find myself going overboard. The tempo at the beginning of the overture was, I fear, a little brisker than it would – or should – have been, had I walked to the platform unaided.)

An equally special occasion was during an Italian tour with the National Children's Orchestra of Great Britain in 2008. This culminated in a performance in the extraordinary open air amphitheatre in Lady Susanna Walton's remarkable house in Ischia, *La Mortella*. Lady Walton was an ebullient hostess. I still remember her dismissing one or two very famous conductors with a few sharp epigrams: 'Cold' for one; 'Lecherous' for another; 'Dull, dull, dull' for a third! It would not be useful for me to identify the objects of her derision, but it definitely made me feel challenged to do my best possible work. Sadly, there turned out to be an open-air discotheque on the beach a mile or so away, heavily amplified, so the orchestra's rather sensitive performance of Delius' *The Walk to the Paradise Garden* was only partially audible. The moral of this is be prepared for the unexpected and to play on regardless. Lady Walton was apologetic afterwards and said kind things about the orchestra, ending with the phrase, 'The Italians are impossible, of course!'

Perhaps my finest performance with a youth orchestra was given in 1985 when I took the combined chamber orchestras of the St Paul's School and St Paul's Girls' School to Her Majesty's Prison Grendon (where I was a prison visitor) in Buckinghamshire on a Sunday afternoon to play part of the programme we were giving at St John's Smith Square in London later that week. We had with us the wonderful Bulgarian violinist, Vanya Milanova, who was playing Beethoven's Violin Concerto, Op. 61. I had wrestled with the issue of which was the right movement to offer to an incarcerated audience. In the end, I came to the view that the first movement was the only one that would be satisfactory, despite its long orchestral introduction and its rather serious tone. Vanya was clearly hugely moved by the sight of over two hundred and fifty men – typically serving sentences of five to ten years' imprisonment – listening to her performance. I do not know what they expected; they would have been in their cells if they had not been at the concert, which probably provided some motivation to attend. What they got was the finest performance I have ever heard given by a solo violinist in any venue in any work; the cadenza was earth-shaking and hugely physical. The prisoners leapt to their feet at the end of the movement, applauding and cheering. I think everybody in the room shared in that moment of intense emotion; for the young musicians, it was an unforgettable experience. We cannot claim that music can always have so powerful an effect, but no conductor should underestimate the potential for a life-changing moment during a live performance.

Guest Conducting

As a conductor, you will hope to acquire some permanent engagements where you are able to develop the technical potential of your ensemble, plan programmes, and develop a long-term artistic relationship. It is likely, however, that some – possibly even most – of your work will be as a guest. Guest conducting has its advantages: musicians tend to be more tolerant of you as they know you will not be with them for long! It is also likely that when you offer some of your personal views of the music, they will have the advantage of novelty as far as the musicians are concerned.

It is wise to remember that, as a guest, you will be able to change the style of the performance by only a limited extent. You can encourage better intonation in a choir but you can only improve the basics of singing technique over an extended period of rehearsal. You can persuade an orchestra to shape their phrases more carefully; you will be unwise to try to change the fundamental sound of a section. There are grey areas: you will come across brass players who use too much vibrato (singers too, for sure!) which seems to you unnecessary or even inappropriate. You can, of course, ask them to rein it in a bit, but many of them may find it impossible to make a totally straight tone. This is particularly true in some countries where 'pure tone' is regarded as simply inexpressive. In such circumstances, it may be unwise to press the issue. In the same way, you will meet basses, both string and choral, whose sense of rhythm leaves something to be desired; again, it would be wise to deal with that reasonably gently; aim for a percentage improvement rather than a life-changing Damascene conversion.

We need to remember the metaphor of the person who dismantles his watch only to find that he cannot reassemble all the pieces in the time available. As a guest conductor, you are most unlikely to have the time to dismantle your ensemble and rebuild it in an entirely different way before a performance. My advice is to try to work with what is there and build on that. It is also unhelpful to begin your rehearsal, or series of rehearsals, by giving the orchestra a lecture on your artistic vision. Leonard Bernstein famously spent ten minutes explaining to the BBC Symphony Orchestra why he had such an affinity with Elgar before beginning to rehearse the *Enigma Variations*. The great broadcaster, Humphrey Burton, made a rather splendid film of that rehearsal which clearly demonstrates the lack of enthusiasm the orchestra felt for Bernstein in this repertoire. It would unquestionably have produced better results had he simply played the work through first and philosophised later. Great conductor though he was, he simply misread the character of the orchestra in front of him.

Auditions

A similar principle applies to conducting auditions. It is always wise to work with what you have rather than try to remake it entirely in a fifteen- or twenty-minute audition. When advising choirs on the appointment of a new conductor, I have often been surprised by the way in which some candidates spend three or four minutes lecturing the choir before they allow any singing. Inevitably, this gives them less time to show their skills and ignores the fact that what the singers want to do, is to sing. A lighthearted quip may be engaging, an extended homily either about music or singing will not be. I remember one particular would-be choral conductor saying to the choir halfway through his audition (which required him to rehearse Britten's *Cantata Misericordium*), 'You're never going to manage to sing this'. I did not need to persuade the choir that he was not the right candidate for them!

The best way to make your first impression upon an ensemble is to be as natural as possible, greet your musicians politely, introduce yourself and start to make music. If you find their first few minutes of music-making impressive and exciting, say so. If you can see a number of problems, start with only one or two and be quick to congratulate them if and when they respond to your suggestions. It is quite surprising how often conductors manage to convey a slight lack of confidence in the musicians they are directing. It is part of any manager's job to convey a sense of belief in their collaborators and a conviction that the ultimate result of their labours will be well worth the effort. Any indication of impatience or insecurity on the conductor's part will ultimately have a negative effect. Sarcasm should certainly be avoided and no musician would wish to be patronised by a conductor who talked down to them. We have to remember our potential for doing harm as well as our potential for doing good. Your fellow musicians, whether amateur or professional, may be sensitive and some possibly insecure; these are common characteristics of many performers. Conductors need to have well-developed radar in order to ensure that they reduce rather than add to the inevitable stress of preparing and presenting musical performances. Unhappy musicians seldom achieve the best results.

A good way to make a favourable impression upon an orchestra is to show clearly that you have looked at your rehearsal schedule from their point of view. Always try to make the best use of the players' time. (See 'Programme Planning', page 21, for more on this.)

Guest conducting abroad

Guest conductors in a foreign country need to adapt to different conventions, different styles of rehearsal and, in some cases, linguistic obstacles. French orchestras, for example, dislike rehearsing in any language other than their own. Scandinavian orchestras are both able and willing to rehearse in English.

My first visit abroad was to the Albuquerque Chamber Orchestra in New Mexico. This came about entirely because I met their conductor, the charming David Oberg, in a restaurant near the Royal Albert Hall after a BBC Prom. We liked each other immediately and, after some correspondence, agreed to an exchange of rostra. The Albuquerque Chamber Orchestra was an interesting mix of local professionals with a number of high quality players who had sought 'The Big Outdoors' after disenchantment with life in a major metropolitan orchestra elsewhere. Prominent among these was Don

Pleznicar, who had been an oboist in the New York Philharmonic. He had had a moment of revelation in his middle age and decided that he wanted a less pressurised existence. To have a player of such quality in a pivotal position in the woodwind section transformed the sound of the orchestra. The players were extremely welcoming. The four rehearsals provided was luxurious by UK standards; I intend the orchestra no disrespect when I say that their speed of work was less rapid than in an equivalent English orchestra – used, as these are, to working under intense time pressure. The final result, however, was admirable. We had time to get to know each other and the music pretty well. A quaint feature was my contract. It was four pages long and included the clause 'The conductor is not permitted to rehearse string players desk by desk'. I never discovered the source of this, but it is certainly something I would never think wise with any orchestra. (Perhaps the most disconcerting moment was driving into the car park for the concert, in full concert mode, to discover a car park attendant, of somewhat hostile mien, sporting a revolver on each hip. Knowing the incidence of violent death in New Mexico, it caused a moment of anxiety!)

I returned to the US twenty years later to conduct Brahms' Requiem in Seattle. Shortly after landing after the ten-hour flight, I found myself taking a chorus rehearsal at the equivalent of 3 a.m., UK-time! In fact the full-throated singing of the chorus and their extraordinary enthusiasm carried me along until the end of the rehearsal. This enthusiasm is an American characteristic; the singers were amateur but splendidly trained and few British choirs would sing with the same physicality. The orchestra, the Bremerton Symphony, was a mixed group of professionals and amateurs, and the string sound, so crucial in Brahms, initially concerned me. However, the extended rehearsal schedule – again, four sessions before the day of the concert – enabled them to develop the sound in a marked manner. These two excursions to the New World reminded me just how absurdly constricted British rehearsal patterns generally are, and how astonishing it is that our musicians routinely give fine performances. Ultimately it is about resolve and money; the British political class has never been fully committed to the Arts, with the honourable exception of Jennie Lee and David Mellor, the two outstanding Arts Ministers of my lifetime.

Of my European trips, two stand out: the Varna Philharmonic Orchestra in Bulgaria and the Iceland Symphony Orchestra in Reykjavík. In Bulgaria the orchestra spoke little English. I had absolutely no Bulgarian although I had prepared a friendly couple of sentences phonetically, which orchestras always seem to appreciate. Luckily, I had a wonderful young translator who, though not a musician, had gone to the trouble of learning a number of musical terms to translate. She was enchanting, though visibly disappointed that I did not use much technical language in rehearsals! The orchestra was fascinating; almost all the string players had been trained in Russian Conservatoires. The sound was sumptuous, and I was pleased to have brought with me Elgar's *Introduction and Allegro for Strings*. The vital solo string quartet sadly suffered from the absence of the principal viola. He had gone off to Turkey for an unspecified time to play in an orchestra that was clearly paying him more money than the pittance the Bulgarians were receiving. The manager assured me he would be with us the day before the concert. This proved to be optimistic; he never appeared. The second viola indicated – without need for a translator – that he would not play the solo part, so the young third viola was shoe-horned into the role. This was not ideal, particularly as the concert was being broadcast live. We all somehow survived but it was a less happy moment in an otherwise lovely evening, with Vanya Milanova giving a radiant account of Brahms' Violin Concerto, Op. 77. As a guest, I refrained from being critical of the wind playing which was circumscribed by the quality of the actual instruments, many of which were in poor order. The collapse of the Soviet system, whatever its other merits, had a very negative effect on orchestral music; subsidies on tickets had been removed so that audiences had fallen and players' salaries had become inadequate. I learned a great deal from those musicians, who had been brought up in such a different tradition.

Iceland was different again. The orchestra spoke very fluent English so I could return to making the occasional light quip with some possibility of it being amusing. They had an extraordinary rehearsal pattern of only four hours in each day. There were many young women in the orchestra; a crèche was provided for their children, and this was clearly an important factor in keeping some of the best players in their home country. When I discussed this with orchestral players in the UK we marvelled at the lack of support here for mothers who are making a career as orchestral musicians. I hope that UK managements are getting better at thinking about this crucial issue.

Practical considerations

As a visiting conductor, there will be practical considerations to bear in mind. If you are driving to your venue, always allow more time than you think you need. It is very difficult to climb out of a car and walk straight onto the platform to begin rehearsing; much better to have time for a cup of tea, to make yourself comfortable in the dressing room and to get a sense of the acoustic of the hall, especially if it is new to you. If you choose to drive yourself, some advance knowledge of local parking arrangements is really useful. If you are rehearsing for the first time on the day of the concert, some idea of where to find an agreeable meal before the 'show' is also useful. You may, of course, be able to be guided by some of your musicians, and even to join them, but you will need to remember that they may feel inhibited if the conductor is sitting with them. They may possibly wish to discuss your shortcomings and will not be able to do so if you are with them!

If there is a pre- or post-concert reception, you will probably be invited and expected to attend. Being enthusiastic to sponsors, to the Mayor or to the Chairman of the Board, are all duties that go with the territory. On the other hand, it is possible to tire oneself unhelpfully in these gatherings. At the launch of the Collins Classic Recording label, I was horrified to see the Spanish conductor Rafael Frühbeck de Burgos standing for forty-five minutes talking to various executives and general hangers-on from Collins before he had to conduct an extended concert. Nobody offered him a chair and he was having to make conversation in his second language just when he needed time to draw breath and settle his mind. It was courteous of him to agree to come to this, but I very much doubt if it helped the performance. Our concert promoters may well pay our fees and rightly expect us to be agreeable to them, but there also needs to be a clear understanding that you cannot begin to perform just by turning a switch. If we have spent the previous half an hour talking affably to a number of strangers, most of us need time to gather ourselves before embarking on a performance.

A final but perhaps obvious point is the journey home. A great deal of adrenaline is likely to be generated by giving a performance; one tends to emerge from the auditorium still full of it. A long drive home is potentially quite dangerous. You will reach a point when your adrenaline level falls away abruptly. I have seen no statistics for the number of musicians who have had accidents on their way home after a concert. Anecdotally, one has heard all too many stories of incidents, some of which have had devastating consequences. Increasingly, my practice has been to drive home the next day if the distance is more than modest, or to take public transport where possible.

Opera and Ballet

Conducting opera and conducting ballet might appear at first sight to be very similar activities; in fact, they are radically different. In the opera pit, it is the conductor's duty to accompany and support the singers. The ultimate choice of tempi rests with the conductor but no sensible musician would adopt a tempo a singer found uncomfortable or unconvincing. With ballet, it is entirely different. The last thing the dancers want is for the conductor to wait for them. They require rhythmic and reliable pulsation to propel their demanding physical movements in a way that enables them to fit their actions to the music and not the other way round. Basically, you should follow the singer but lead the dancer.

Collaboration

What opera and ballet have in common, of course, is the requirement to collaborate with artists from different disciplines on equal terms. You will hope, or even optimistically expect, that your opera or ballet director will know and love the music. This hope will not always be justified and there have been many occasions when conductors and directors have fallen out, which is most unhelpful both from the point of view of other performers and from that of the audience. Nonetheless, in my experience, most professionals want to collaborate amiably and not many put their ego in front of the artistic endeavour.

In February 1992 I conducted for a visiting French ballet company – *Le Ballet du Nord* – for a week at London's Sadler's Wells Theatre. The company had given performances in five provincial centres before coming to London but always with recorded music. Happily, they had decided to use live music for their London appearances and engaged the Wren Orchestra and the City of London Choir to provide it for them. I was delighted to be asked to conduct though I was not entirely convinced that the main work chosen – Mozart's Requiem – was a wise choice for a ballet. The other two works, Stravinsky's *Apollo* and Dello Joio's *There Was A Time* were established ballets and provided an intriguing musical counterweight to the Requiem. Both were new to me and I enjoyed getting to grips with the scores and indeed, programmed them subsequently for string orchestra concerts as both are quality pieces.

In many ways, it was an enjoyable week. To conduct the Mozart seven times in five days was a marvellous experience though not very comfortable for the choir who were squashed into the pit around the outside of the orchestra. The soloists sat on the opposite edges of the front of the stage which worked well. However, the basic problem was that the director, JeanPaul Comelin, had learned the work from the second Karajan recording that the maestro had made fairly near the end of his life. Some of the tempi were exceptionally slow, quite possibly for other reasons than purely musical ones. In particular the tempo for the 'Hostias' (which Mozart marks 'Larghetto') was a ponderous Adagio. The dancers hated it and were delighted when I moved it forwards to a more mainstream tempo. Monsieur Comelin was livid. I asked him gently what other performances of the Requiem he had heard; it was clear that the answer was none. There evolved a nightly ritual of his assistant, an affable American, coming to see me after every performance complaining that my tempo for the 'Hostias' was insufficiently slow. I am afraid I could see no way of adopting a tempo that felt so much against the rhythm of the harmony. Each evening I replied that I would do my best to move it backwards a little, but that neither the dancers nor the music would be better served by the extreme tempo of the recording that the director happened to have purchased when he was learning the piece. By the final day, the director had clearly crossed me off his Christmas-card list and he failed to come back stage to say farewell. By that time, however, he was also locked in conflict with the orchestral manager because he had erected a pair of microphones to record the orchestral performance without consulting the players or the manager. I was relieved that he had opened a second front which gave his assistant other negotiations to contend with.

Happily, I have always had cordial relationships with the other ballet directors with whom I have collaborated. (I particularly enjoyed one whose method of travel across a rather large stage area was on a very glossy, chromium scooter!) Inevitably, however, all of us will occasionally experience tensions with collaborators in our performances. My guiding principle is that soloists, whether instrumental or vocal, must always be provided with the tempo they require, but that non-musicians, however distinguished, cannot expect to overbear the conductor's judgment on matters of tempo. An interesting middle ground arises with a record producer, of course. Many of them are excellent and highly experienced musicians. It would be foolish of a conductor to ignore a piece of advice from such a source without weighing it up very carefully.

Practicalities of rehearsals

Another major difference between ballet and opera is that the singers seldom wish to use their full voice at rehearsals, even sometimes at the dress rehearsal. Ballet dancers, on the other hand, always seem to commit a hundred per cent to the physicality of their movements. When they got to Sadler's Wells, it transpired that *Le Ballet du Nord* dancers had not been paid for a month, but there was not the slightest slackening in their commitment and energy. Indeed, they asked if they could go on for fifteen minutes after the orchestral rehearsal had finished to sort out an uncertain moment of choreography. I was happy to play the relevant section on a piano while the players were leaving the pit. Musicians do not generally provide unpaid overtime!

The opera conductor is wise to go to most, if not all, of the piano rehearsals to help form a clear view of what is happening on the stage in the performance. This can sometimes inflect the musical interpretation notably if the singers have a lot of action on stage when they may find it hard to sing out to the audience. As a student, I marvelled to see the great tenor Gerald English singing Richard Rodney Bennett's opera *The Ledge* in the foetal position for most of the work. I cannot remember who the conductor was but he or she must have required extraordinary sensitivity to the needs of the singer to ensure that the words could be heard by the audience. Regrettably, there are conductors who take less care of their singers than this. Drowning the singers – and thereby depriving the audience of the text – is a cardinal sin and one that singers do not lightly forgive.

Visibility needs to be at the forefront of your mind if you are in the pit. Orchestras may be cramped but they can generally see the conductor reasonably well; the singers on the stage may find it harder. In some performances, I have had the luxury of closed-circuit television that enabled singers with a limited view from the stage to see the beat easily on a screen. In this situation, you need to be mindful that your beat is within the visual field of the camera; nothing is more frustrating than to have the conductor's beat disappear below the screen when a singer is searching for guidance. Even without television, you may need to raise the beat higher than you would normally do, so that your singers can see clearly. Sometimes, those on stage cannot hear the orchestra clearly; one should be sympathetic if a singer – who is performing entirely from memory – asks for a little more help from the conductor. To counteract the danger that the orchestra will be too loud for a particular soloist onstage, I strongly recommend going into the auditorium at least a couple of times to check that the balance is as you have imagined. One can sometimes have an alarming surprise in that situation.

In my very early days, I conducted Mussorgsky's *Boris Godunov* at Cranleigh School with a mixed cast of professional singers and senior students. The chorus included boys from the school, a contingent of girls from St Catherine's School, Bramley, and – rather splendidly – a group of trainee Catholic priests from the local seminary! There were obvious problems of balance with the large, and mainly professional, orchestra. We solved them at a stroke, by placing the orchestra behind the stage. This was only possible, of course, because the stage was being specially constructed for the performances. The school was also happy to invest in television screens for the stage – not a very frequent occurrence in the 1970s. Cranleigh had a great tradition of performance; Michael Redgrave had been on the staff in the 1930s and given some memorable Shakespearian performances. This made it easier to deploy substantial resources to subsidise opera and the result was that some London newspapers came to review the school's productions. I often feel that having the orchestra behind the singers could be a real advantage. Peter Knapp, the singer/director, quite often placed his orchestras – already reduced – behind or alongside the stage. Whenever I conducted for his shows, one could hear from the audience's response that his excellent English translations of Mozart and Rossini were being clearly heard and enjoyed. There was no need for any surtitles in his productions!

One of the great things, of course, about working in the theatre is that you generally have more than a single performance, whereas most symphonic concerts give you only one opportunity to get things right. I have always envied actors their luxury of multiple performances as I have seldom left the platform without wishing that I could perform the work again the next day. That is why touring, with all its stresses and discomforts, is so often rewarding.

Sir Adrian Boult conducted regrettably little for opera, although the evidence of his late recordings of Wagner is that he would have been a formidable Wagnerian. It was a happy coincidence, however, that the last time he conducted for a live audience of any kind was a performance of Elgar's *The Sanguine Fan* ballet at London's Royal Opera House. In view of all the obstruction he suffered from Sir Thomas Beecham, he must have left the pit (I think his presence was not announced to the audience, for some reason) with some sense of fulfilment. Those who were there were exceptionally fortunate; I wish I had been one of them.

Recording

Making a recording is quite a different skill from that of live performance. There are, indeed, some conductors who have a particular skill at producing outstanding recorded performances but are much less outstanding in a live situation. Financial resources for recording used to be relatively generous; in the 1980s, for a sixty-minute CD, one would normally have four or even five sessions of three hours each to create the record. The pressure of pirated recordings, free downloads and platforms such as YouTube and Spotify have made the financing of classical recordings much more difficult. Nowadays, many recordings are made with only three three-hour sessions and even world-class orchestras often require sponsorship to make a recording of anything other than the most overtly popular material. All of this places intense time pressure on the recording sessions; this requires the conductor to be extremely efficient in delivering a good recording in the shortest possible time.

The role of the producer

I have always taken the view that the conductor should leave issues of balance to the producer, once he or she is satisfied that the basic orchestral or choral sound has been established. Rushing into the control room to hear extracts wastes precious studio time and is better done in the rehearsal breaks or between sessions. A good producer will have a very clear picture of how much you need to achieve in any individual session and a wise conductor accepts such guidance gracefully. Additionally, a good producer, including most BBC producers, will be skilled at managing conductors in the studio. If one gently suggests to you that a slightly different tempo or balance might sound better on the recording, it would be manifestly unwise to reject it lightly.

I prefer to record relatively long stretches of music at a time. I only resort to two- or three-minute extracts when there is a specific fault that must be rectified. It is undeniably true that there are some recordings where an impressive result has been achieved by stitching twenty-bar fragments together; that is a triumph of the producer's skill but not, perhaps, of the conductor's art.

The editing process

Many conductors feel that their work is over once the final session is ended. I do not agree with this. Of course, you will be invited to comment on the final edit but I have found it far more productive to spend time in a studio with the producer, refining the first edit into the final version. Some producers are highly skilled musicians. Andrew Walton, for example, who has produced many of my most convincing recordings, was a professional violinist, so he understands the sound of the orchestra 'from the inside'. I still find it very useful to listen to his first edit with him so that I can question any passage that gives me concern. Very often, he is able to 'tweak' the sound to move it closer to my ideal. Back in 1988 when I recorded *The Evening Watch* (for Hyperion's

Helios label, see 'Discography', page 93) – a collection of terrific but neglected music by Holst – it was only when listening to the first edit that we uncovered a sudden drop in pitch near the end of the very challenging title piece of the disc. Martin Compton, another excellent producer, performed some miracle of digital magic, and happily the issued disc had no such lapse! I am not a fan of 'auto-tuning', however. You can always detect it, if you know what to listen for, and its artificiality seems to dehumanise the performance.

Of course, many new possibilities have been opened up by modern technology. My Military Wives Choirs' recordings (see 'Discography', page 93) have always been made with almost all 2000 singers taking part. The recordings are made at regional centres, however, with two or three hundred singers at each session. The producer Sean Hargreaves (who had introduced me to this remarkable network of choirs) and John Haywood then stitched the recordings together with additional instrumental performers in the studio; the results are a triumph. As a conductor, one still makes a contribution, but one's success is very much in the hands of the wizards in post-production.

The 2020 COVID-19 pandemic gave fresh value to technological skills. Many choirs – including the City of London Choir, made video recordings in which each singer recorded themselves at home, watching an on-screen conductor. They then passed their individual recordings to a producer who made an ensemble performance by electronic means. Some of the results were surprisingly convincing. I prefer the live interaction between musicians and conductor 'in the flesh', of course. Nonetheless a most moving video was issued by the Military Wives Choirs in conjunction with Westminster City Council of 'Abide With Me' to the famous tune *Eventide*. I had conducted a performance to camera; a number of Military Wives singers came to the studio at various times and sang to the video of my beat. Somehow, it all worked, and the emotion generated by the video is very powerful. All conductors will need to adapt to the ever-increasing range of technological possibility, but we are not yet close to robot conductors, and we must hope that such are not imminent.

One always needs to remember that a recording is a permanent statement about the conductor's view of a particular work at a particular time, so it is worth taking a great deal of trouble to achieve the best possible outcome. That said, one's view of the music will, of course, evolve over time. I now listen to my recording with the London Philharmonic Orchestra (LPO) of Mozart's 'Jupiter' Symphony No. 41, K. 551 with a strong sense that the slow movement is quite simply too slow. It is marked 'andante cantabile' which clearly suggests a flowing, forward movement. Pushing the conductor in the opposite direction are the very large numbers of demi-semiquavers that embellish the melodic line and lead one to a more stately tempo. Moreover, I had a relatively large string section for this recording which also required a little more space between pulses. Nonetheless, with hindsight, I am clear that my tempo is fundamentally too slow and I am almost unable to listen to the performance because of that. Perhaps the moral of this story is that one should avoid too much retrospection with one's recordings (in much the same way that reviewing past relationships is seldom productive!).

The Mozart disc was made for Collins Classics who were just embarking on their rather short-lived foray into recording. I was fortunate to be invited to conduct three of their initial ten discs for them. These included Holst's *The Planets* suite and an Elgar disc, as well as the Mozart (see 'Discography', page 93). All three discs were made in three sessions only. The LPO's playing was marvellous in all the repertoire; it was during a golden period for them, and they were hugely responsive and helpful. It is a great shame that *The Planets*, which is perhaps my best recording and was one of the choices of the Penguin CD guide, was deleted by a new team recruited only twelve months after it was issued. The Mozart, on the other hand, remained available until the label was sold on after heavy losses several years later, and was reissued on their cheaper 'Quest' label. One of the ironies of conducting a recording is inevitably that you have very little control over its ultimate use.

Online music platforms

Inevitably, modern recording is further affected by the presence of online music platforms. A number of my recordings can be downloaded for free, without my agreement, but one is very reluctant to make much fuss about it as I would surely prefer the recordings to be available than not. The violinist Tasmin Little has eloquently testified to the tiny rewards she has received for hundreds of thousands of downloads of her outstanding performances on Spotify. Demonetizing recorded music is a genuine danger for the future of high-quality classical performance. If the music-loving public come to believe that high-quality performance can be free, musicians will not be able to make a living and the profession will contract. This is an issue that successive governments have failed to address and one of the most urgent challenges of twenty-first-century Western music. I hope a solution will be found in my lifetime!

Contemporary Composers

It is a responsibility of all performers to act as a bridge between living composers and their potential audience. This is not always as easy as it might appear; orchestra and choir committees and their managers tend to be conservative – mainly because the financial implications of new music are often alarming. Audiences can be resistant to new music, and part of the job of the conductor is to act as an advocate for contemporary composers whose work deserves to be heard.

First performances

First performances can be among the most exciting events in a conductor's career. Thoughtful repertoire pairings can help to overcome any audience resistance and add an extra frisson to everyone's experience. In a Milton Keynes Festival in the 1980s, we paired Richard Blackford's newly-composed *English Mass* with Rossini's *Petite Messe Solennelle*; it gave both choir and soloists two different sets of challenges but the audience had a varied and exciting Sunday afternoon. A decade later, a large-scale piano concerto by David (Dave) Heath entitled *Passion Unleashed* wonderfully played by Piers Lane, was paired with Britten and Holst, which helped to fill the auditorium and gave the audience palpable excitement. I also commissioned a major choral work from Stephen Oliver, *Prometheus*, in 1989. It was an imposing piece: his personal and passionate protest against the UK's Conservative government's attempt to anathematise homosexuality. However, Stephen made what I believe to be a mistake in choosing to set the majority of the piece in ancient Greek. That decision inevitably made it harder for the power of the music to communicate to the audience in London's Royal Albert Hall; its pairing with Walton's *Belshazzar's Feast*, with its splendid and vivid English text, sold out the hall but in hindsight, did the new piece scant favours. Nonetheless, *Prometheus* deserves more exposure and I hope that it will one day be championed by another conductor. The end, in which the words 'They can never kill me' are repeated in multiple languages, is deeply moving.

The central challenge for the conductor in programming a new work is that you are required to 'sell' the piece, not just to the audience, but also to the performers. Of course, that is true when you conduct any unfamiliar work, but the symphonies of the English romantic composer Cipriani Potter, though unknown, use a Beethovenian language with which an orchestra will readily identify. Of course, when playing from parts that have not been used for over a century, there may be similar problems to those of a brand new piece. When I recorded two of the Potter symphonies, there were wrong notes in the parts that needed attention at rehearsal, but it was fairly straightforward to identify what the right notes should be. In a new contemporary work, one will often need the composer to be present at rehearsal to ensure that the written notes are those intended. Occasionally, it will become obvious that the composer has not got a detailed grip on exactly what was intended, which can be a vexing moment for the performers!

During his period as chief conductor of the BBC Symphony Orchestra (1930–1950), Sir Adrian Boult probably conducted more new works than any other conductor in the twentieth century. He always prepared with assiduous care, even when he did not care for the work in hand. No composer ever got a bad first performance from him, but it is probably true that his willingness – derived from a powerful sense of duty – to take on anything he was asked to do, led to some slightly dull performances where he simply could not convince himself of the quality of the music.

As a conductor, you will be regularly solicited by composers asking for performances. I have found that honesty – carefully filtered through politeness – is the only way to respond to a virgin score. If you pretend to enthusiasm, any reasonable composer will bombard you with the question, 'when are you going to do my piece?'. It can be exhausting to have to try and find a new excuse every few months for non-delivery; it is surely better to say that you do not feel that you are the best person to give the first performance. There have been embarrassing occasions where conductors and composers have fallen out publicly before a first performance and these are unhelpful to both protagonists. Sir William Walton was overtly scathing about Sir Malcolm Sargent after the Leeds premiere of his *Gloria*, and the relationship between Sir Michael Tippett and Boult was seriously overshadowed by the famous incident in the premiere of Tippett's Symphony No. 2 when the piece came to a halt. With characteristic integrity, Boult took responsibility, but it is now generally accepted that the fault lay with a dispute over the barring patterns between the composer and the leader of the BBC Symphony Orchestra at the time, Paul Beard. Accidents will always be possible in a complex new work, especially with the limited rehearsal time many British performances provide, but it is generally better to keep going at all costs so that most of the audience, at any rate, do not grasp that something is seriously amiss. Orchestral musicians are particularly good at maintaining continuity under pressure if they do not believe that the conductor is the source of the problem – and sometimes, even when they do!

One of the best ways to avoid any moments of stress in the first performance is to ensure that you have ample time to talk to the composer before you get anywhere near the ensemble you have to direct. This is true even if you are doing an often-performed piece by a living composer. The notes – whether the notation is conventional or not – only tell you part of the story. A clear understanding of what is in the composer's mind is particularly necessary for a first performance. The composer should also be very welcome at rehearsals, as long as interruptions for minor details are kept to a minimum. It is probably sensible to ask the composer to withhold any comments until the break in the rehearsal so as not to interrupt the flow too often, though this may not always be possible. Some composers go almost too far in the other direction by expressing almost no views at all. Karl Jenkins, who has always been a most charming guest at my rehearsals, very seldom makes any comment!

I will refrain from naming composers who insist on a lengthy philosophical monologue before the rehearsal starts, but they are all too real. Certainly, queries over wrong notes are much better directly passed across to the author rather than being left to the conductor's detective skills. Composers with the aural abilities of Stephen Oliver or Richard Blackford can instantly tell you if there is a misprint in an orchestral part; those who cannot hear it may have to accept one or two dubious accidentals.

Not all composers have a clear understanding of what is practical. On one occasion, I conducted a broadcast of 'second performances' with the BBC Concert Orchestra. The slow movement of a tripartite sinfonietta provided the horn section with not a single rest of any duration at any point. The principal horn enquired tartly, 'Has this piece had its first performance?'. I reminded him that all the works were, indeed, having second hearings; 'Why this one?', he replied. Luckily, the composer was not present in the control room so I was able to smile affably rather than finding myself obliged to defend the piece. Harmless as the piece sounded, this technical incompetence made it hard to convince the orchestra that their time was being well spent in rehearsing it.

Choral premieres

Choral premieres can be even more challenging than orchestral ones. The late twentieth century brought forward a number of composers who effectively invented new choral sounds to communicate their message. Some of these were strikingly effective; others less so. When presenting them to an amateur choir, the conductor frequently needed to be able to demonstrate some of these sounds, which was often a real challenge. Composers such as Luciano Berio and Phillip Glass require substantial amounts of extra preparation time which often militates against programming such music – interesting though it can be.

Contemporary composers now write in such an astonishing variety of styles that a conductor must be ready for almost anything when a new score arrives. Unless all your singers have perfect pitch, some modern choral works require weeks of preparation; others with a more tonal language may employ complex rhythmic patterns and multiple time signatures. All these things require extensive preparation from the conductor. It is wise, therefore, to beware of taking on too many new works simultaneously unless you have an exceptional memory. Vernon Handley had a particularly detailed capacity for new scores and gave outstanding first performances as a consequence; he generally set aside extended chunks of his summer holiday to work on them, which must have been challenging for his family. Sadly, conductors often require forbearance from their family. In the book *A Life in Music*[2] there is a telling comment about David Willcocks from his daughter, Sarah de Rougemont, who said she only discovered he was very witty after joining the Bach Choir, which he conducted!

---

2 *A Life in Music: Conversations with Sir David Willcocks and Friends* (Oxford University Press, 2008)

Stepping in at short notice

It is in the nature of live music that you may be asked to step in at short notice for any repertoire. This is always slightly challenging, unless it is a piece well-established in your repertoire, but particularly so if it is a new work. In 2011, The London Mozart Players had a special concert on Remembrance Day in London's St John's Smith Square, where they were collaborating with the excellent chorus of Portsmouth Grammar School – with whom they have a continuing and very fruitful association. The conductor was due to be Gérard Korsten; sadly he was taken ill while conducting in the United States a week before the concert and I was asked to take over. The programme was quite testing, including Britten's challenging *Variations on a Theme of Frank Bridge*, but the centrepiece was a requiem by Stephen Montague that had been commissioned by Portsmouth Grammar School. The score was delivered to me two days before the pre-concert rehearsal. The piece is forty minutes long and is for full orchestra, SSAATB chorus, soprano soloist, organ, four fog horns and three off-stage ensembles: three bass drums at the back of the hall, a percussion group on either side of the audience playing wine glasses, as well as hand-held percussion played by students. This was to be the London premiere so there was much interest in the performance. A conductor in this circumstance has some advantages: all the other performers will recognise that he has come in at short notice and will be more than usually tolerant of the occasional uncertain gesture. They will try to be as friendly and helpful as possible. That said, they will be no more familiar with the piece than you are, so the need for clear technique and an effective rehearsal strategy will be even greater than usual.

Such events can be career-changing. Vernon Handley was asked to step in at the Royal Festival Hall with the London Symphony Orchestra in place of André Previn when he was barely known in London. He was almost certainly asked because there was a substantial new piece by Alun Hoddinott on the programme; Handley was known to be exceptionally good at learning scores under pressure. The performance of the new piece, together with Sibelius' Symphony No. 2, Op. 43, attracted much critical notice and moved Handley's career from the second division to the first in one evening. Sir Andrew Davis, while in his early twenties, stepped in at similarly short notice to conduct Janáček's *Sinfonietta*, again in the Royal Festival Hall. He had given a fine student performance in Cambridge a year or so earlier. Word must have reached the orchestral management and this was enough to launch his professional career: the rest is history.

The moral of this is a simple one: be prepared for anything! A conductor needs to be careful, however, not to take on something that is clearly beyond them. Early in the 1980s, I was asked to conduct a rehearsal of Richard Strauss' *Burleske* with the Philharmonia Orchestra when the concert conductor had over-taxed himself and needed a day off. Although this was far from a contemporary work, it was very little known; it was virgin territory for me and most of the players. The request came at 6 p.m. the day before the session and I was already booked to rehearse another group that evening. That left only the morning to get the piece into my head: it was not enough. The Philharmonia were kind and tolerant but it was clear to both them and me that I was not adding anything terribly significant to their rehearsal. It was not crucial, but nor was it helpful to my future collaborations with the orchestra. With hindsight I should have declined – the players would probably have appreciated the afternoon off!

In conclusion

One of the happy outcomes of first performances can be, obviously enough, that one makes friendships with fine composers whom one might not otherwise come to know. Stephen Oliver became a close friend; indeed he was embarked on a small-scale opera to match *Dido and Aeneas*, of which I was due to give the first performance, when he very sadly died. He had written so little of the piece that there was nothing that could be done with it – a source of deep regret to me. Jonathan Dove, too, has become a genuine friend and I learned a lot about the compositional process from him when he wrote fine works for Tonbridge School and for the educational charity The Classical Road Show. 'Keeping friendships in good repair' was one of Stephen Oliver's catch phrases; it was one he lived out in practice – exactly as he did his political beliefs. It was probably John Dankworth who became my closest composing friend, however. He was strikingly generous to me, requiring commission fees only when there were funds available, and helped me to understand better how jazz rhythms work. Whenever he wrote in a more conventional idiom (his three unpublished songs written for the Holst Singers with flute solo are very fine part-songs in the twentieth-century choral tradition), he was always interested in my suggestions, and indeed often discussed his choice of texts with me.

My final conclusion is that every conductor should seek out new works to conduct, commission pieces whenever funds are available and recognise the special advocacy role the conductor requires for a first performance. Only by doing this will music remain a living art form.

The Conductor and the Audience

The relationship of a performer and his or her audience is a fascinating one. At one level, the performer – whether singer, instrumentalist or conductor – is bearing their soul to a group of strangers. At another level, there is a powerful bond between them as the musician leads each audience member individually along a journey constructed for them by the composer. The fact that the conductor is, in one sense, the 'silent musician', while at the same time, the most conspicuous figure on the stage, is another curious contradiction.

All of this is obvious, but it does raise a number of issues for the conductor. I have already mentioned my deep belief that the conductor's gestures should be largely for the benefit of the musicians in front of them rather than the audience behind them. On the other hand, if there is a fascinating dialogue between two or three instruments, or group of instruments, to show this by gesture may well help the audience's understanding of the music. One of the biggest problems for those of us who believe deeply in the power of music is that some of the greatest examples are rather complex. Unlike commercial music, they do not reveal all their secrets at one hearing. Yet the idea that you need to be 'Touched by the Music Fairy' in order to enjoy a Beethoven symphony is manifestly nonsense; it is just necessary to listen with open ears.

During the 1990s, I conducted and presented a programme on Classic FM entitled *Masterclass*. We had an orchestra in the studio and most of the programme was devoted to an introduction to a standard work, or movement of a work, followed by a complete performance. Many listeners wrote to tell me that they found this deepened their understanding of the particular music that we subjected to this process. Interestingly, though the programme had an average audience of 350,000 listeners, there was only one occasion when it conspicuously augmented the live audience for a concert as a consequence. This was a performance of Victoria's six-voice Requiem, which I rather shamelessly used as a featured work a couple of months before the Holst Singers sang the piece in St George's, Hanover Square in London. The audience was twice what we would have anticipated! On the other hand, when Classic FM actually broadcast a concert by the Milton Keynes City Orchestra from the Queen Elizabeth Hall (QEH) on London's South Bank, the audience was little more than we would normally have expected. A possible explanation of this may be that *Masterclass* had a more attentive audience than the breakfast and drive-time programmes on which Classic FM advertised the QEH concert.

The twenty-first century, with its pursuit of instant gratification, does not easily embrace an art which really requires repeated performances to make its fullest impact. Conductors need to be conscious of the responsibility they have to present the score faithfully to their audiences; they must also do all in their power to make every individual performance into a special event. Those who have paid money, and often made a long journey to come to the concert, deserve no less. A conductor who ignores the audience or uses it simply to reinforce personal vanity betrays the trust of the listeners. There is a famous story of Sir Malcolm Sargent emerging from the Artist's Entrance at the Royal Albert Hall with the words, 'Only the first six autographs, I'm afraid' – to which the doorman replied, 'There are only three people here, Sir Malcolm'!

In the audience will be those who know a particular piece well, those who have never heard it before, and many who fall between those two extremes. Somehow, the artist has to speak to all three constituencies on behalf of the composer. This should not encourage us to distort the music in an artificial way but it does require the most intense commitment from every performer on the platform. At the heart of that endeavour, the conductor must strain to make that happen at every performance. Uniquely among musicians, a conductor has not only to give of their very best, but also to persuade a large number of other musicians to do the same.

When things don't go well

Inevitably, not every performance in a 'live' situation will be as good as you would have wished. In a recording, it is often possible to achieve something close to perfection if you have a skilled producer and a sound engineer with enough time to distil the best takes of tricky passages in the music (see 'Recording', page 72). Good recordings are wonderful things but the spontaneity of a live performance trumps any recorded one. If the sparks begin to fly (in a positive way!) in a live situation, the experience both for players and audience is one of the most intense available to us. This will not happen often but the prospect of it keeps us all going and compensates for the long journeys, the cold rehearsal halls and the struggle to find somewhere decent to eat in an unfamiliar town.

I strongly recommend not overexamining a performance that has not gone very well. It is a debilitating process and only useful if it helps to identify moments when you failed to deliver what was needed. To learn from one's mistakes is important and wise; to dwell on them is almost always unproductive and demoralising. It is even more fruitless to discuss errors with your colleagues. There are conductors who have been known to send notes to their colleagues, critiquing some aspect of their contribution to a concert; I think this is a most unhelpful policy. If you are going to say anything to your fellow musicians backstage after a concert, confine yourself to expressing your thanks and wishing them a safe journey home. The music profession is a relatively small one in the UK. Inevitably, conductors are discussed – not always in flattering terms – and the conductor will need a certain thickness of skin.

The audience's response

The audience's response to our work is another issue. Occasionally, it may not be flattering. The final concert in the Milton Keynes City Orchestra's tour of the Eastern United States in 1994 was in the fabulous acoustics of New York's Town Hall. The hall was packed and I came off the platform with a feeling of satisfaction. A number of strangers greeted me outside my dressing room with inspiriting enthusiasm. In the middle of this group of well-wishers was an elderly but bright-eyed woman who greeted me with the words, 'I heard Copland conduct that *Hoedown* piece. He did it faster than you!' I was suitably deflated. (Whether it has actually changed my tempo for that piece, I am not so sure.) However, generally speaking, those who take the trouble to greet you backstage will be more flattering.

Pre-concert talks

If you are a resident conductor, you may get to know some individual members of your audience very well. I have always been enthusiastic about the concept of 'pre-concert talks'. Those who attend will learn something, both about the music and about your human qualities; unless you manage to alienate them, this will help them to engage with your work in the performance. Working so closely with the Guildford Choral Society meant that I often attended post-concert parties, where I met many audience members and formed happy friendships with some of them as a consequence. In Milton Keynes, with a regular subscription audience, we also got to know our most enthusiastic supporters there extremely well. I was frequently invited to supper before concerts; this was a bit of a mixed blessing as I prefer to be silent for the hour before the concert. On the other hand, supper after the concert, though intrinsically more enjoyable, might mean a very late home-coming if one were not staying locally. These are first-world problems but if you are working for two or three consecutive nights, they are worth bearing in mind.

The Classic FM *Masterclass* concept transfers well to the concert hall. The problem with it is marketing. 'Introduced Concert' is not an alluring sales pitch; 'Lecture Concert', even less so. With the London Mozart Players we tried a different tack: 'Get In' was the title and these one-hour, early-evening events were prefaces to a full-scale evening concert a little later in the season. Feedback from the audience was hugely positive; sadly, the numbers were disappointing – often fewer than twenty-five per cent of those coming to the main event. The most successful was my introduction to Vaughan Williams' Symphony No. 5 (in my view, one of the greatest British symphonies) where the percentage of the audience attending went over twenty-five per cent for the first and only time. On the other hand, the audience for the concert was smaller than average!

Despite the relatively low numbers, I still believe the general idea of a pre-concert talk is a good one. An articulate conductor can help an audience to deepen their experience of a piece by providing significant aural signposts. In my experience, the collaboration of the orchestral players has always been wholehearted. Somehow, we must come up with a better way of enticing audiences to engage more deeply with the music, simply so that their own experience may be more intense. No one who has watched Bernstein's films with the New York Philharmonic can doubt this.

The written programme

Another small consideration is that of the written programme. My normal practice was to write a brief welcome at the beginning of a programme, even if I was a guest conductor. I always try to avoid writing programme notes as such; it is a lot of work and if your name is attached to the note, you invite a tiresome message from someone pointing out some error of fact. Speaking from the platform before a little-known piece or a first performance is different. This is very helpful for at least some of the audience and helps to humanise the conductor. Most of what the audience sees is your back view; they are entitled to a little respite from that, at least from time to time!

Attracting audiences of the future

The open-air concert, which tends to have a number of shorter pieces rather than the conventional programme with its overture/concerto/symphony pattern, is easier to market than concerts regarded as 'highbrow'. Conducting large numbers of these with the Wren Orchestra taught me the key role of the conductor as presenter as well as interpreter. We had over 4,000 people for a performance of Bliss' *A Colour Symphony* in the grounds of Kenwood House; in London's Royal Festival Hall, 500 would have been a considerable achievement. I briefly introduced each movement separately; the audience appeared to appreciate that and certainly showed much enthusiasm at the end. Of course, that enthusiasm may have been partly related to the bottles of wine being consumed by some! Nonetheless, those open-air events attracted many people who would not go to a more formal concert in an auditorium. I always felt frustrated that it seemed so difficult to transfer these huge and enthusiastic crowds into the Royal Festival Hall for a more formal concert.

Precisely the same principle applies to the splendid concerts put on by the Raymond Gubbay organisation. These are formulaic events, but the formula works. Large numbers of people who would not go to a Royal Philhamonic Orchestra or Philharmonia subscription concert do come to 'The Last Night of the Autumn Proms', where they manifestly enjoy themselves. These concerts have always required the conductor to interact with the audience much more than in a traditional concert situation. Typically, there are at least six pieces in each half and the audience expects Elgar's first *Pomp and Circumstance* march as the finale. There are musicians who sneer at this; I emphatically do not. Any door that leads to the magic garden of the love of music should be opened enthusiastically. What is challenging is the difficulty of enlarging prom audiences' horizons beyond the Gubbay formula into a wider search for musical excitement. The many thousands who love the 'Nimrod' movement would almost certainly enjoy the entire *Enigma Variations* as well. A desire to put things into neat pigeonholes somehow obstructs this upward movement; I have only had marginal success in my own career in challenging these stereotypes.

It is also important to develop a young audience. Most major orchestras now have excellent outreach programmes and I have much enjoyed conducting short concerts specifically aimed at school or family groups. A great deal depends upon finding the right tone with which to speak to your audience (an essential feature, in my view). I am not entirely convinced by a new tendency to bring in some popular artist as a compère who has a limited genuine enthusiasm for the repertoire you are going to conduct. Someone with real enthusiasm for the programme is more likely to be convincing. The programme also has to be carefully chosen, of course. Short works are better than longer ones, but all the music need not be loud and rhythmic; I have often used J.S. Bach's 'Air' from his Orchestral Suite No. 3 in the middle of a concert for young people and had a wonderful sense of quiet throughout. Music that has an obvious programme – Dukas' *The Sorcerer's Apprentice* or Dvořák's *The Noon Witch* often makes a powerful impact. The educational charity, The Classical Road Show, has a programme for secondary schools called 'The Front Row Club'. This involves providing free tickets for a group of Year 10 and 11 students who sit in the front row of whichever venue is chosen. I, generally in company with any soloists, visit their school once or twice before the event to introduce the music and set the scene. The enthusiasm of almost all those who have attended these concerts has been palpable. None of these projects are, in themselves enough, of course. What is needed is a much greater investment in school music; this is something that has been sadly neglected by governments for over thirty years.

The future, dominated as it clearly is by social media, is quite hard to read. We know that celebrity is a twenty-first-century obsession; we know that glib categorisation is the basic marketing tool; we know that most people prefer to function inside their comfort zone. The plain fact is, however, that the best of Western classical music speaks of the fundamentals of human experience. Research by Classic FM has shown that someone who goes to a classical concert for the first time is only marginally more likely to go to a second than if they had never attended. If they go to two, they are ten per cent more likely to go to a third. Once they have attended three, they are seventy per cent more likely to go again. This is a vital piece of intelligence for all of us who believe in the power of great music to change lives. Exactly how we push people past the magic number three is the key issue. It is one I have struggled with all my career and I do not yet have a clear answer; I am still searching!

Odds and Ends

Despite some professional orchestral players' views to the contrary, conductors are members of the human race. They are subject to the same weaknesses, temptations and personality flaws as we all are. Unfortunately, the conductor is very conspicuous by the very nature of the role. This leads me, not without hesitation, to offer some advice which may already be obvious but is often ignored.

Alcohol

All performers live their life under the pressure of stresses engendered by their occupation. It is very easy to use alcohol as a stress management tool; it is always a mistake to do so. Boult was well known to be virtually teetotal; Beecham derided him for this but it is likely that his exceptional longevity as a working conductor was partly a product of his lifestyle. There are conductors who are known to be alcohol dependent; inevitably, it lessens the respect in which they are held by performers. If you drink before a rehearsal or a concert, you may feel things have gone well, but you may be mistaken. Though that can be true of any performance, there is no denying that one's critical faculties are diminished by alcohol.

Sometimes, of course, you may confront the issue with your players rather than yourself. I came onto the platform in the Civic Hall in Guildford in 1982 after the interval to conduct Orff's *Carmina Burana*. Having bowed to the audience and full of anticipation at the dramatic beginning of the piece, I turned to the orchestra to discover the trombone section was not present. It transpired they were still in a nearby local pub; I had to leave the platform and wait while they were hastened back to their seats by the orchestra manager (this was before the use of mobile telephony). The audience may have been unaware of the cause of their lateness, and even somewhat amused by it, but it put the performance at risk and made our working relationship difficult. In the twenty-first century, this kind of incident has become less likely but even now, there will be choir members who may sneak out for a drink in the interval of a rehearsal; this needs to be strongly discouraged.

This may all sound unattractively puritanical but our duty to our audience is a serious one and the conductor is responsible both for his own and for his musicians' conduct. This is not something about which you would lecture your musicians from the rostrum, but you may need to discuss it with an orchestra or choir manager if you see an incipient problem.

Appearance

Conducting is a physical activity and you are quite close to your front desk players. Leonard Slatkin, in his excellent book, *Conducting Business[3]*, tells a self-deprecatory story of going out to lunch with two of his principal players, shortly after becoming principal conductor of the St Louis Symphony Orchestra. He asked them how they felt things were going; their first response was to invite him to use a stronger deodorant. Few players in an English orchestra would be that candid but conductors need to be self-aware in this area as well as in so many others. It is also a matter of basic courtesy to players and singers to take trouble with one's appearance and with one's personal hygiene. One does not wish to see one's front desk string players trying to move backwards during a rehearsal!

Punctuality

A conductor should not keep players waiting for the beginning of the rehearsal. Occasionally, there will be some disaster – a major accident on a motorway for example – when ones loses control of this, but one should try to build in some contingency time to every plan. Just as it is wrong to seek to conduct with inadequate preparation, it is wrong to overfill your diary so that you are not certain to be able to fulfil your commitments. I once saw Pierre Boulez rehearsing Stravinsky's *The Rite of Spring* (a piece he was capable of conducting from memory), at 10 a.m. in the Royal Albert Hall having been driven there directly from Heathrow airport after an overnight flight from Japan. He was manifestly struggling with jetlag; the orchestra did not like this and had every right to resent it. I have learned (rather too slowly, perhaps) not to overestimate my own stamina. An orchestra or choir does not wish to know if you are exhausted, unwell or stressed. They expect you to get on with the job and if you are not able to, they will feel that you should have stood down. This may sound harsh but it was explained to me exactly in those terms by an orchestral violinist in Belfast when I was trying to conduct a complex work (Liszt's Piano Concerto No. 2) with acute sciatica.

Relationships

The social relationship with your players or singers is another potential minefield. To keep yourself aloof invites an impression that you think you are too important to be friendly with your musicians. Too much familiarity, on the other hand, may be equally irritating. Many professional orchestras do not really want the conductor in the pub with them after a rehearsal but an amateur choir might welcome it, and indeed, be disappointed if you disappear too quickly. This is, perhaps, the core of the difference between amateurs and professionals. If you play or sing on a full-time basis for a living, it is simply impossible to imagine that every rehearsal or concert is going to engage your full enthusiasm. For enthusiastic amateurs, however, it is rather different. Such estimable musicians are giving up time – and often paying money – to do what

---

[3] *Conducting Business: Unveiling the Mystery Behind the Maestro* (Amadeus Press, 2012)

they love. In such a situation, conductors must ensure that they maintain and enhance this enthusiasm. All musicians prefer to achieve their best standards rather than fall below them, but all conductors who direct an amateur group are well advised to remind themselves that those they are directing could easily do something else if they do not find rehearsals enjoyable.

It may just be useful here to stress that conductors need to be careful of their personal behaviour because of their very exposed position. Several conductors have made happy marriages with orchestral members; Bernard Haitink is a conspicuous example of this. This is not unique to the music profession; many doctors marry nurses. It is not unusual to be attracted to people who share your interests and understand your work. The need for caution is nonetheless obvious; in the present climate, too much caution is far wiser than too little. A conductor may also have to deal with fallout from relationship difficulties within their orchestra or choir; particularly on tours where people can behave unwisely. The conductor is unlikely to be a trained therapist or a counsellor, although some may seek to use you as one, but a need for compassion and sensitivity is common to all leadership roles.

Agents

In the age of websites and instant communication, it is entirely possible to make a career without an agent. Many of my engagements have come from personal contacts. The major function of an agent is to negotiate fees, which is always more difficult to do for yourself. I have had three agents, all of whom have become friends and whose advice I have frequently sought. On the other hand, they will have to forgive me if I say that only a minority of my engagements have come through them. By far the most significant was a contract from the Hungarian National Philharmonic Orchestra which my present agent, Patrick Allen, brought to me in 2020. Ironically, it fell victim to COVID-19 along with so much else. The moral of which is that even agents cannot control epidemics!

Of course, if you become a major international figure, you will want your agent to take complete control of your diary so as to avoid double-bookings. I have had a few of those myself and they are obviously infuriating as well as embarrassing. Much depends upon one's personal organisation skills; mine have limitations and I rely upon my part-time personal assistant to keep some kind of grip on the organisational aspects of my career.

Social media have become greatly more significant in the lives of musicians in the last two decades. A dinosaur like myself will always be behind his children in social media skills, but I have learnt to use Facebook and Twitter to publicise concerts and to keep in touch with some of my audience. It is quite fun to give an audience your Twitter handle at a concert and see how many new followers you have in the next few days. As in the case of Malcolm Sargent (see 'The Conductor and the Audience', page 80), it is less delightful if there are only three!

Critics

People sometimes ask me if I read reviews of my concerts. The simple answer, is yes. Of course, if the review is negative, or even lukewarm, it is upsetting. I try to use such reviews as an educational tool, though sometimes it is possible to discern some subjective element in the response. Inevitably, one is more affected by the negative than the positive, though an enthusiastic notice does perk one up considerably. When I recorded the Samuel Wesley symphonies with the MKCO, Stanley Sadie wrote a generous review in *Gramophone* magazine which clearly helped sales and reassured me that these works were genuinely undervalued. Taking both negative and positive reviews in one's stride is nonetheless the best way to deal with critics; over time, one tends to find that things even out – not unlike umpiring decisions in cricket!

Health

Conducting is good aerobic exercise and there is some evidence that conductors can expect longevity if they do not misuse alcohol or drugs – or eat unwisely. On the other hand, conducting does put strain on the back and you may find yourself standing more or less still for several hours in a performance. This alone is an argument for economy and restraint in gesture, aside from all the other practical considerations I have mentioned earlier. Even with a controlled range of gestures, however, back problems are an issue for many conductors. How to manage this is clearly a matter of opinion. Some people do regular back-strengthening exercises, others put their faith in osteopathy (of which Boult was a great advocate). For myself, I have always found a good masseur is the best solution. Easing muscular tension on a regular basis is a good stress-management technique in any case; if it is also keeping the back supple, that is an obvious advantage. When I was conducting in Iceland, the hotel provided me with an exceptional masseur. While he was unlocking my back on the day of the concert, he said, 'Now I am looking after you, tonight you will look after me!' This turned out to be a charming way of telling me that he had bought a ticket for my concert!

A conductor also needs to be mindful of the condition of the feet after a long day's rehearsal on a hard platform. One's evening shoes are inevitably less supportive than trainers, but your feet need to be comfortable. Ensuring that your shoes do protect your feet from the pressures of extended standing is simply common sense.

Family life

The musician can be a demanding family member. You are often away at the weekends and in the evenings, which are conventional family times. The distinguished organist, Peter Hurford, had a particularly demanding schedule in the 1980s; when he came to play concertos in Milton Keynes in 1989, he brought his wife, Pat (who was a long-term friend of mine), to turn pages for him. We had an interesting conversation after the concert; she said, 'You musicians want meringues and massage when you come home. What your wives want is some decent conversation!' I am afraid that there is more truth in that than there should be. I have learned from three wives and six children that the important thing is to make time for your family whenever you can. In particular, I recommend respecting family holidays, even if they conflict with an attractive professional engagement.

Lady Boult was assiduous in protecting her husband from unwelcome visitors, the press and, sometimes, even his students. Frequently, she would also bring him milk in the interval of a rehearsal. In the twenty-first century, of course, most spouses will, rightly, have their own professional careers so that this level of support is not only unreasonable, but impossible. It is, nonetheless, always a bonus to have one's family at a concert. This serves to remind me, of course, that it is important also to support one's children's concerts whenever possible! Work-life balance has become a hot topic in recent years; a conductor has to be particularly careful not to lose sight of this. Most musicians are driven people; music is an absorbing profession and it is not always easy to see one's life objectively. Reviewing one's diary on a regular basis is a necessary discipline and one I recommend without reservation.

Coda

This little book, despite its anecdotal quality, is primarily concerned with aspects of the conductor's art and technique. However it must not be forgotten that the fundamentals of all music-making apply as much to other performers as to the conductor. The conductor's leading role does mean that their work can have a profound influence over those with whom they interact, whether fellow musicians or audience. Nonetheless, basic issues of style and interpretation are the same whether there are two or two hundred performers.

The conductor needs to lead and manage fellow musicians. This should not mean micromanaging people who know more about the detail of what they are doing than the conductor does. Even if exceptionally gifted and knowledgeable, a conductor is still the servant of the composer and should place the written text above all personal vanity and self-regard. All conductors need to beware of seeking, even unconsciously, to exploit their power and to behave in a dictatorial manner. The conductor may be primus inter pares, but autocracy is not a good model for music-making. Of course, conductors like Fritz Reiner and George Szell, who deliberately bullied and intimidated their orchestras, would not nowadays be tolerated, but it is still possible for a conductor to make players or singers feel insecure. To do so is to betray the trust musicians should have in their conductor. Studies have shown that many orchestral players attribute much of the stress of their professional lives to conductors; this is something none of us should regard with equanimity.

My experience of the greatest conductors whom I have known is that they are always endeavouring to discover new beauties in the great works of art that they are seeking to interpret. Sir Adrian Boult, Bernard Haitink and Sir Colin Davis were all looking for ways to improve their understanding of scores, however many times they had previously performed them. Sir Simon Rattle continues to present himself with new musical challenges, both of contemporary and period performance. Self-criticism is a vital quality in a conductor and someone bereft of it will never serve the music as well as it requires.

My suggestions about conducting technique are, of course, not universally agreed. Any reader of this book can go to any major concert hall and see much of what I suggest being contradicted from the beginning to the end of the concert; some of the performances may, nonetheless, be first class. This obviously raises the question as to whether *any* technical skill is really required. I believe the answer is a resounding 'yes'. Power over the performance can be exercised by a conductor with rudimentary technique who manages to overcome this with sheer musicianship, concentration and force of personality. Most of us, however, will do much better with an expressive and effective technique that enables us to be helpful even if we cannot always produce an exceptional performance.

Three score years and ten used to be regarded as the target lifespan for humanity. Nowadays, there are many conductors in their eighties still doing marvellous work. Herbert Blomstedt, who at the time of writing is ninety-four, continues to show us how simplicity and economy allied to unselfish service to the composer, produces the best results. This puts conductors in a privileged position. We should be improving all our working lives; if we are fortunate, we have rather longer than most musicians to go on improving. The goal then is to ensure that our range of expression and depth of intellectual grasp of the music broadens and deepens throughout our career. Of course, this makes it more likely that our best performances will be of music we have done many times before. Nonetheless, we should challenge ourselves to new work on a regular basis so that we are not in danger of rather complacently repeating performances that we know we can do well. The spectacle of an international conductor flying from one country to another, repeating the same small repertoire for exorbitant fees is an unedifying one, but sadly far from unknown.

All musicians can provide inspiration, healing and spiritual stimulus to our audiences. The conductor is almost unique in being able to do the same for his musical colleagues. Very few people can manage that all the time but even to be able to provide it for some of the time is an enormous gift. It is one that we should be careful not to take for granted. At the end of the day, making music with other people is one of the most rewarding experiences available to us. Looking back over my long and varied career, I can remember a few occasions when I wished I had stayed at home, but the overwhelming memory is of joy in music-making. To all professional colleagues, aspirant conductors and indeed audience members, I would simply say: never lose sight of the transformational power of music. Great art may be mankind's finest achievement; we have never needed it more.

Acknowledgements

Many people have helped to make this book possible. Some are mentioned in the text, but there is a core group without whom it would neither have been written nor have reached the public domain. I am particularly indebted to my dear friend, Paul Harris, proprietor of Queen's Temple Publications, for commissioning the book and to his splendid editor, Leigh Barnett, whose patience, understanding and forbearance were extraordinary. Her expertise was of considerable assistance at many points. My long-term friend and personal assistant, Melanie Bowesman-Jones, took endless trouble to ensure detailed accuracy of the text, while my son, Alexander – himself a skilled conductor – read the drafts and made helpful comments.

I am also very grateful to Alan Rusbridger, who has been kind enough to write a preface at exactly the same time that he was clearing his office at Lady Margaret Hall, Oxford, and moving house – a true gesture of friendship. I consulted a number of my professional colleagues over details; Sian Edwards, with whom I taught conducting at the Guildhall School of Music and Drama, was a particularly insightful source of advice. Her students at the Royal Academy of Music, where she now leads the conducting course, are very fortunate to have such a wise guide.

Though there is no guarantee that he will receive my thanks, it will be obvious from the text that it was Sir Adrian Boult who formed much of my understanding of conducting and, indeed, of the potential of music to change lives. I owe him much; I could not have had a better mentor. I hope that I have managed to pass on to my own students something of what he gave to me.

Finally, special thanks go to my wife, Professor Tonia Vincent, and my sixth and final child, Eleanor, who were exceptionally tolerant of my absence from meals and other events, while I wrestled with the text – particularly during the coronavirus lockdowns. Tonia's help was invaluable, particularly because her detailed and perceptive comments on the text were informed by her experience of singing as a member of the City of London Choir.

Discography

Various Britten Choral dances from Gloriana; Bliss Pastoral 'Lie strewn the white flocks'; Holst Choral Hymns from the Rig Veda *Holst Singers and Orchestra*	Hyperion 1985
Vaughan Williams Five Tudor Portraits & Five Mystical Songs *Guildford Choral Society*	Hyperion 1988
Holst The Evening Watch & other choral works *Holst Singers*	Hyperion 1989 Reissued 2004
Raff Symphonies Nos. 3 and 4 *Milton Keynes City Orchestra*	Hyperion 1989
Mozart Symphony No. 41 'Jupiter' & Eine Kleine Nachtmusik *London Philharmonic Orchestra*	Collins Classics 1989 Reissued 1993
Elgar Enigma Variations; Chanson de nuit; Chanson de matin *London Philharmonic Orchestra*	Collins Classics 1989
Cipriani Potter Symphonies 8 & 10* *Milton Keynes Chamber Orchestra*	Unicorn-Kanchana 1990
Mendelssohn Symphony No. 1 & Symphony No. 5 *Milton Keynes Chamber Orchestra*	Unicorn-Kanchana 1991
Vaughan Williams Mass in G Minor; Festival Te Deum *Holst Singers*	Unicorn-Kanchana 1991 Reissued by Regis Records 2003
Wesley Symphonies 3, 4, 5 & 6 *Milton Keynes Chamber Orchestra*	Unicorn-Kanchana 1991
Sterndale Bennett Concerto No. 4; Fantasia in A; Symphony in G minor* *Milton Keynes Chamber Orchestra*	Unicorn-Kanchana 1993

Crotch Symphony in F; Organ Concerto No. 2; Overture in G; Symphony in E flat* *Milton Keynes Chamber Orchestra*	Unicorn-Kanchana 1993
Holst Choral Symphony & Choral Fantasia *Royal Philharmonic Orchestra* *Guildford Choral Society*	Hyperion 1993 Reissued 2002
Holst Choral Ballets *The Philharmonia* *Guildford Choral Society*	Hyperion 1995
Parry Job *Royal Philharmonic Orchestra* *Guildford Choral Society*	Hyperion 1998
Vaughan Williams Hodie & Fantasia on Christmas Carols *Royal Philharmonic Orchestra* *Guildford Choral Society*	Naxos 2007
Various In Terra Pax: A Christmas Anthology *Bournemouth Symphony Orchestra* *City of London Choir*	Naxos 2009
Beethoven Der Glorreiche Augenblick; Choral Fantasy *Royal Philharmonic Orchestra* *City of London Choir*	Naxos 2012
John Gardner Cantata for Christmas; Organ Concerto; Christmas Carols *The Holst Orchestra* *City of London Choir*	EM Records 2012
Various Flowers of the Field *London Mozart Players* *City of London Choir* *Roderick Williams*	Naxos 2014
Various Home for Christmas *Military Wives Choirs*	BMG 2016
Haydn Mass In Time Of War (Paukenmesse) *Royal Philharmonic Orchestra* *City of London Choir*	RPO 2017

Various The Nation's Favourite Carols *Royal Philharmonic Orchestra* *City of London Choir*	Classic FM 2017	
Various Remember: 12 Pieces For The Centenary Of The 1918 Armistice *The Band of the Household Cavalry* *Military Wives Choirs*	2018	
Michael Stimpson The Angry Garden & Silvered Night *Royal Philharmonic Orchestra* *City of London Choir*	2019	
John Gardner The Ballad of the White Horse & An English Ballad *BBC Concert Orchestra* *City of London Choir* *Ashley Riches & Paulina Voices*	EM Records 2020	
Various Military Wives Original Motion Picture Soundtrack *Military Wives Choirs*	2020	

*Denotes world premiere recording